Succ Cacti

FRANZ BECHERER

Series Editor
LESLEY YOUNG

MEREHURST

Contents

Mamillopsis senilis from the mountains of northern Mexico.

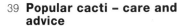

The flower of a Lobivia pentlandii.

Melocactus with a cephalium.

Introduction

At first glance, cacti, which are often hardy, spiny, tough plants, are not nearly so attractive as, for example, exotic orchids – yet, year by year, they continue to conquer hearts and inspire affection among those who grow them. It is true to say that cacti are more capable of arousing a collector's passion than almost any other family of plants. So, what is their secret? Perhaps it is their bizarre shapes. Or is it their ability to transform, almost overnight, from a rough, prickly, bare stem into a radiant, flowering beauty? Whatever the attraction is, it must be obvious to everyone that cacti are very different from other plants and will, therefore, require a different kind of care. Many a newcomer to cactus growing is surprised at the fact that they seem to flourish, yet refuse to flower and, for the beginner, this will spoil their enjoyment of these exotic plants. Very often, it is simply minor mistakes in care that prevent one from experiencing the beauty and splendour of the cacti flowers.

All you need to know about the successful care of cacti is explained in this colourful guide. Expert advice and clear instructions on buying, positioning, care and propagating will ensure that these "spiny children of the desert" feel right at home on your windowsill or in your greenhouse, so that they will flourish and produce magnificent flowers.

The author, Franz Becherer, a cacti expert of some 30 years' standing, himself owns something in the order of 10,000 cacti. His lovely colour photographs are designed to introduce you to the most beautiful cacti, and he provides detailed instructions on the care of individual genera. For this purpose, he has chosen cacti that will rapidly oblige with successful flowering, even for the beginner, because it is surely the goal of every cactus lover to create a "living desert" in their home at least once a year. One important prerequisite for this is correct overwintering and, here, the author provides precise and clear instructions on the most important points. He also gives competent advice on the proper care of cacti all year round, whether you are watering, fertilizing, providing the right soil or misting and spraying. Step-by-step colour illustrations clearly demonstrate all the necessary procedures. The author also shares tips, culled from his own experience, on how to handle and repot cacti without injury to oneself. Please make sure that you read and absorb the important instructions on page 63, which will alert you to the risks associated with handling cacti.

Even though they are very robust, cacti can become infested with pests and diseases. With the help of colour photographs, you will be able to identify such problems and treat them successfully with tried and tested methods used by the author.

One whole chapter is dedicated to the particularly fascinating subject of propagating and grafting. You will be surprised to find out just how many ways there are of propagating cacti, and how simple they are. The well-tested advice offered by this experienced author will make it easy for the beginner to grow and care for cacti successfully and to coax them into producing flowers. However, even the more experienced cacti lover will surely find a few new hints and tips to enrich his or her own knowledge of these rewarding plants.

The lovely colour photographs, which were specially taken for this guide, show how enchantingly beautiful cacti can look if they are well cared for.

The author

Franz Becherer, a collector and raiser of cacti for 30 years, started out with a few cacti on his windowsill and gradually extended his collection through the use of balcony boxes, cold frames and small greenhouses. He has been the proud owner of a large greenhouse for eighteen years, and this now contains some 10,000 cacti, partly in a large bed (see photo, inside back cover). He has been a member of the Deutsche Kakteengesellschaft (German Cacti Society) for 25 years, as well as a founder member and committee member of many years' standing of his local branch of the German Cacti Society.

Bright as the desert sun
A flower of Echinocereus roetteri showing the green stigma so typical of Echinocereus. The diameter of the flower is about 6 cm (2½ in).

All about cacti

The cacti family must surely include some of the weirdest and most individual creations in the entire plant kingdom. The enormous variation in shape and form found among cacti is truly amazing and almost infinite. They range from the inconspicuous, tiny *Blossfeldia liliputana* to the giant "bellies" of *Echinocacti,* often weighing several tonnes, and the candelabra trees of *Carnegiea gigantea*, which can tower to heights of 20 m (65½ ft).

The cacti family

Cacti and certain other plant families together make up the group called succulents. This term is a collective name for plants that are able to store water in the cells of their stem tissue or in their leaves. Linnaeus's name *Cactus* was the origin of the name for the family of cacti (*Cactaceae*) which today includes some 200 genera. Of these, around 14,000 species have been described, although the internationally recognized number of species is thought to be more like 2,000.

The origins of cacti

Cacti are "Americans". If they are found growing wild in any other continent of the world today, this is because they have been introduced by people. In their original homeland, where they occur naturally, they are found from the Peace River in Canada to the very southernmost tip of continental South America. They grow along the coasts of the great oceans and right up into the Andes mountains, to altitudes of almost 5,000 m (16,400 ft). They are able to survive in the scorching sands of inland desert landscapes as well as in inhospitable, barren, rocky plains or when battered by the snowstorms of the Rocky

Mountains, the Andes and the altitudes of Patagonia. Some species have adapted to life in tropical areas, where they hide under bushes, climb up trees or grow in pockets of leaf humus in the forks of trees in rain forests (epiphytes). It is a constant source of amazement to discover how perfectly adapted different cacti species have become to the climatic conditions of their habitats: some manage to survive on water derived from mist and fog or on extremely rare rainfall,

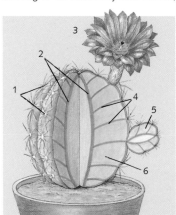

Parts of the cactus
1. areoles; 2. central bundle of vascular tissue; 3. flower; 4. side bundle of vascular tissue; 5. offset; 6. water-storing tissue.

while others manage to live under metre-thick falls of snow. However, cacti do not occur in equal concentrations in the entire 12,000-km (7,500 miles) long area of their distribution. The greatest concentration of species is in the arid regions of North and South America, around the tropics of Capricorn and Cancer. Most of them occur in the southern states of the USA and in Mexico, northern Chile, Peru and Bolivia.

What are cacti?

Cacti are veritable masters of adaptability. They have secured their survival in hot, arid deserts and rocky terrain by changing the elements of their structure (for example, their leaves). The extremely arid regions of present-day America evolved about 60 million years ago – during the Tertiary period. The rule of survival for any plants living here was to absorb lots of water and store it without losing very much at all through evaporation. In the course of their evolution, such plants had to adapt all the main components of their physical structure – roots, body and leaves – to the existing and often extreme local conditions. The result of this adaptation is the cactus. The great variety of shapes and forms found in cacti is quite fascinating, yet they all share the same basic design.
The roots of individual species are quite differentiated, however, depending on the conditions of the habitat to which they have had to adapt.
● Large turnip-like roots are particularly able to store water. This type of root can be found in cacti that inhabit rocky deserts or in flat-growing species that grow prostrate and have bodies that can store only small amounts of liquid.
● A widely spreading root system, situated just below the surface, is a

Echinocactus ingens – a heavyweight globular cactus.　　*A wild Cylindropuntia bigelowii may grow 3 m (10 ft).*

characteristic of all cacti that are at home in sandy areas or flat, dry deserts. This root system is best able to take advantage of brief, heavy showers of rain.

● Epiphytes are characterized by a heart-shaped root system.

● Climbing cacti grow aerial roots in addition to other roots.

The body of a cactus is a "storage tank". In order to prevent the loss of moisture through evaporation via the surface of its skin under the scorching sun, cacti have come up with a novel adaptation: the top layer of skin (epidermis) is very tough and leathery. Small, slit-like openings, which can be opened or shut, depending on the surrounding temperature, control the cactus's water balance. Some species protect themselves from the effects of intense sunlight with a bluish wax-like layer or by growing cork-like

layers on their skin or velvety, fluffy or woolly flakes on the surfaces of their bodies, not to forget the dense spines and hairs which envelop most cacti and provide shade for their bodies.

Flowers may appear after two or three years in some cactus species but other species do not produce them until they have attained a certain size or age. This is the reason why some species, when cared for by humans, only rarely, or never, display their flowers (for example, *Cephalocereus senilis, Carnegiea gigantea*). Still, you can count on the fact that cacti that have flowered at least once will regularly flower again, given the right kind of care. Cactus flowers are very short-lived (they often flower for just one day or night), but are breathtakingly beautiful (see photographs, p. 28). They utilize the entire range of the

colour spectrum except for blue as the genetic component for this colour is missing. In addition to the brilliant colouring, there is the huge range of flower sizes: from tiny flowers only a few millimetres across to the giant flowers of "Queen of the Night" (*Selenicereus grandiflorus*) which have a diameter of up to 40 cm (16 in).

The physical structure of all species of cacti is very similar, however (see illustration, p. 32). Pollination occurs by the transfer of pollen grains from the anthers to the stigma. How to do this by hand is explained in the chapter on propagating and grafting (p. 32).

The growth of the spines – the "fingerprint" of a cactus

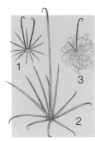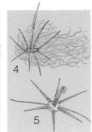

The appearance of the spines around the areole is typical of each genus, sometimes even for a species. 1. typical Mammillaria areole; 2. Glandulicactus uncinatus; 3. Mammillaria bocasana; 4. Oreocereus celsianus; 5. Ferocactus recurvus; 6. Gymnocalycium quehlianum; 7. Thelocactus bicolor; 8. Mammillaria plumosa.

The cephalium – a fascinating innovation!

Some cacti genera announce their imminent flowering – usually at the age of about seven years old – by. developing a cephalium. This compact accumulation of bristles, hair and wool is the flowering zone of the plant from which the flowers will form

● A genuine cephalium is only formed by *Melocacti* and *Discocacti* species (see photo, p. 3). The cephalium sits like a little crown on the top of the body. As soon as it has formed, the green body of the plant ceases to grow.

● A pseudocephalium (a false cephalium) is found in columnar cacti. This forms when the cactus is ready to flower, grows downward from the growing tip of the shoot and then carries on growing upwards, together with the rest of the plant. The pseudocephalium is usually produced on one side only – the side facing the sun – but a second one occasionally appears on the opposite side.

Just like the cacti themselves, **the fruits and seeds** are very varied. After pollination, the flower will begin to fade, the ovary will swell and seeds will develop inside it. **The fruits** are often equipped with regularly spaced cushions of spines whose purpose is to protect them and which are sometimes not formed until the ripening phase. The ripe, spherical to oval fruits may be inconspicuous. Some are hidden within the body of the cactus, others are coloured a striking, brilliant orange or red and may attain the size of a hen's egg. Many are juicy, fleshy and edible by animals and birds (not people!). Some may split open along their side; others remain closed like berries and drop off the parent plant when ripe. Others, again, do not release their seeds until they are ready to drop, and then shed them via a hole situated at the stalk end of the fruit.

When ripe, **cacti seeds** are usually dark brown to black. Only a few *Mammillaria* possess light brown seed husks. One fruit may contain up to several hundred individual seeds.

The spines: It is a biological fact that cacti have spines and roses have prickles – even if the cactus has been called "a prickly customer" and the saying goes "never a rose without a thorn". The spines are the adapted leaves of the cactus but the surface of these leaves has been reduced to an absolute minumum. This is a very sensible adaptation as the larger the leaf surface is, the more moisture is lost by the plant through evaporation. A further advantage is that the cactus is protected by its spines from being eaten by animals. Some species have spines with tiny hooks (or barbs) attached to them, which help with propagation as they are able to catch on the fur of an animal and be carried to another location. Some are even capable of absorbing moisture from the air in the form of dew. The spines are situated around the areoles (see illustration,

More about cacti

Areoles (see illustration, p. 6) are woolly cushions of spines at the tips of the warts or tubercles, on the surfaces of the protuberances or on the edges of the ribs. Flowers and offsets grow out of the areoles.

Axils (for example, in *Mammillaria*) are depressions between the warts or tubercles. These often possess hair or wool just like the areoles.

Bundles of vascular tissue (see illustration, p. 6): These are the "scaffolding" of every cactus body and run vertically like an inner column through the entire body of the cactus. They consist of tough fibres which conduct water and nutrients from the roots to the tissues and to the growth zone at the crown of the plant (shoot).

Lateral vascular tissue (see illustration, p. 6): This branches off from the main bundle of vascular tissue and supplies the shoots (offsets) and flowers at the areoles and axils with water and nutrients.

Offsets (see illustration, p. 6) are new shoots that appear out of the areoles or axils.

p. 6). This combination of spines and areoles together is a typical characteristic of each individual cactus species.

If you look closely, you will see that every areole has two types of spines:

● The spines around the edge are directed towards the body of the plant and often envelop it.

● The central spines are usually larger and tougher and protrude outwards.

If you take a good look at the spines of a cactus, you will be surprised by their colours and variety. The illustrations (see p. 8) and photographs (see p. 11) will give you a good first impression of this. In addition to the plant's physical elements, as mentioned above, there are a number of other features which every cactus lover should know about (see table, p. 8).

Shapes of growth

Many people think of a cactus as being "something round and prickly". Basically, they are right, as numerous cacti adopt this spherical shape in their youth. However, with increasing age, they may develop column-like, tree-like or bush-like shapes, or create entire clumps or cushions by growing shoots. If cared for indoors or in a greenhouse, however, many species may never develop beyond an advanced juvenile stage.

The following basic shapes of growth can be identified (see illustration, right).

Tree-like cacti, occasionally with metre-tall, thick stems which do not branch out until they attain a certain height from the ground (for example, many *Cereus* species and *Carnegiea gigantea*).
Cultivated cacti: Usually only column-shaped; will not form branches until the cactus has reached a certain height.

Bush-shaped cacti with several equi-sized stems or a short main stem which rapidly forms branches (for example, *Cleisocactus, Peireskia* and some *Opuntia*). In some species, the extended shoots "tip over" and carry on growing in either prostrate or pendulous form (for example, *Haageocereus, Aporocactus*).
Cultivated cacti: First a single stem grows upwards, often followed from below by small groups of shoots, like organ pipes.

Spherical (globose) cacti are the most widely distributed type and may often grow into a truncated-pillar shape. Some (for example, *Astrophytum, Echinocactus*) remain solitary, others form shoots from their base (for example, *Echinopsis, Lobivia, Notocactus, Parodia,* many *Mammillaria* and *Echinocereus*).
Cultivated cacti: as in the wild; when they form shoots they will form only small clumps.

Cacti which form clumps and cushions from their multi-branched shoots. These short, semi-spherical cushions may cover an area of up to several square metres (for example, *Echinocerea* and *Mammillaria*).
Cultivated cacti: have a short lifespan; grow as solitary plants but also in groups or clumps.

Climbing cacti have long shoots and branch out into bush-like shapes (for example, *Selenicereus, Hylocereus*).
Cultivated cacti: may be tied to a tall support or to a round frame.

Epiphyte cacti possess leaf-shaped, long-limbed shoots and grow into bushy groups, which may attain a pedulous shape (for example, *Nopalxochia, Pyllocactus, Rhipsalidopsis, Schlumbergera*).
Cultivated cacti: grow as in the wild.

Unusual growth

Cacti may grow in shapes that deviate from the normal shape of their species because of genetic mutation. These are referred to as "monstrous shapes".

Cristates may look very different, depending on the species. In this case the shoot tip of the cactus broadens out in a band and forms strange, tortuous shapes because of stress that occurs during growth (see photo, p. 14).

Dichotomous division can occur in *Mammillaria*. When this happens, they divide across the top so that usually two, but sometimes three or four, heads are formed which then fuse together. This division may continue.

Mutations may occur in seedlings.

   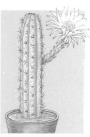

Shapes of growth of cacti
1. Epiphytic growth – leaf-like linked pads which grow in a bushy fashion.
2. Bush or tree-like growth, for example, in some Opuntia.
3. Globular or spherical shape which may begin to stretch with age.
4. Columnar shape which may branch out with age.

Among these are the chlorophyll-free forms of *Gymnocalycium mihanovichii* and *Chamaecereus sylvestrii* which can only be kept alive by grafting them on to another robust and healthy cactus.

Terminal flowers: The top of the cactus grows into a flower, which signals cessation of growth for the plant.

Cactus names

If you wish to take up growing cacti, you will not get very far without knowing their scientific names (usually Latin or Greek in origin). Only very few have common English names. (For example, *Astrophytum* = bishop's mitre; *Schlumbergera* = Christmas cactus; *Cephalocereus* = old man's head.)

The scientific name of a cactus usually consists of two parts: the generic name and the species name (plus, if appropriate, the variety name).

For example: *Echinocactus grusonii var. albispinus*

The generic name is *Echinocactus* (= spherical cactus). This is followed by the species name: *grusonii* (= named after Gruson), and the variety: *var. albispinus* (= white-spined variety).

A brief history of cacti

In Europe, the history of cacti did not begin until the discovery of America by Christopher Columbus in 1492. Columbus was the earliest known European to encounter this new plant form when he took his historic first step on to the sand of a West Indian island and found himself among *Melocacti*. He must surely have brought some of these strange-looking "melons", with their armour of spines crowned with a bristly cap, back from the New World, as, by 1535, Spanish reports give exact descriptions of these cacti. A British apothecary displayed a *Melocactus* (see photo, p. 3) as a special rarity in his collection in London in 1570, possibly descended from that first consignment of cacti brought back by Columbus. Later explorers of the Americas brought other spiny plants to Europe and, by 1700, melon, columnar, foliage and fig cacti were known in Europe. The Swedish naturalist Linnaeus described 22 species of the genus *Cactus* in his first work on systematic botanical classification, *Species Plantarum*, in 1753. In the course of the exploration of the New World, a constant stream of newly discovered plants was brought to Europe.

The Victorian era: Cacti collecting fever reached a peak during the early to mid-Victorian era, until palms, lilies, orchids and chrysanthemums took over.

In Germany, research into cacti was initiated by Prince Fürst zu Salm-Reifferscheidt-Dyck (1773-1861) who visited botanic gardens all over Europe and brought together specimens of all the existing cultivated succulents in Europe in one of the largest collections in the world at his palace in Düsseldorf. He worked out a classification system for cacti and left many scientific works to posterity.

Later inventories: As cacti fever began to fade away, valuable collections were dispersed and many rare plants were lost. It was not until 1892, when the Deutsche Kakteengesellschaft (German Cacti Society) was founded, that the low point of cacti interest in Europe was reversed when K. Schumann, a professor of botany, wrote his *General Description of Cacti*. The renowned cacti expert Curt Backeberg (1894-1966) travelled extensively in the countries of origin of cacti and wrote numerous books. His six-volume monograph *Cactaceae* and his *Kakateenlexikon* (Encyclopedia of Cacti) are, to this day, the only reference works on cacti approaching anything like comprehensive studies. Professor Buxbaum also wrote works on their morphology and researched their classification system, while American botanists called Britton and Rose compiled a four-volume monograph called *The Cactaceae* in 1920.

After 1918: After the end of the First World War, a merciless campaign of environmental exploitation began in the homelands of cacti. Without any sense of responsibility, cacti hunters brought masses of plants across the ocean to Europe where most of the plants died due to a general lack of knowledge about their care.

With the outbreak of the Second World War, cacti were temporarily forgotten until a post-war increase in the western world's standard of living reawakened an interest in cacti. Nurseries had been involved in the sale of cacti since 1900, of course, but they usually dealt with imported plants. During the last few decades, professional cultivation has become increasingly established, so that, gradually, there has been less and less need to import cacti anymore. Nowadays, collecting cacti is organized both privately and through national and local societies which are to be found all over the world.

Spines – protective but beautiful

The appearance of cacti is colourful and very indiosyncratic.

1. *Echinofossulocactus*: The dagger-like central spine is very typical. The individual species can be identified by means of a "spine key".

2. *Mammillaria geminispina*, with a wild-looking, very sharp and black-tipped array of spines, produces many offsets and forms unapproachable cushion-like structures.

3. *Mammillaria guelzowiana* has treacherously soft-looking, velvety fluff concealing short, tough, yellow to black "fish-hook" barbs.

4. *Thelocactus hexaedrophorus* possesses brilliant red spines.

5. *Navajoa peeblesiana* is able to absorb moisture from the air via its cross-ribbed, curved spines.

6. *Uebelmannia buiningii*, from the Brazilian jungle, spreads its spines over lumpy ribs.

7. *Thelocactus rinconensis* has short spines arranged in a triangular formation with a thick, black base.

8. *Ancistrocactus scheerii* has a dense coat of spines, with black-brown-yellow, barbed central spines.

9. *Astrophytum senile var. aureum* has pliable spines which are yellow near the top of the plant and envelop the entire body of the cactus.

Buying cacti and initial care

Cacti, which are generally quite tough customers, seem to follow their own rules in many respects. When you are buying cacti, therefore, you must forget everything you ever knew about other plants. Cacti with flowers, for example, are by no means a guarantee of the good health of the plants – and if you buy cacti in winter you may be in for a great disappointment.

Where to buy cacti

Wherever you happen to buy a cactus, make sure it is named.

Garden centres, flower shops and nurseries generally do not sell cacti they have grown themselves, but plants they have ordered from large cacti growers. The choice can sometimes be amazingly large.

Special cactus nurseries will often sell their plants straight from the greenhouse or by mail order. They will generally have a very large selection of species on offer, will be able to give you good advice and you should be certain of obtaining a properly cultivated cactus specimen. If you order cacti by mail order, you should be aware that they are only sent during frost-free periods and without a pot.

The plant and flower sections of large department stores and other venues will often offer a surprisingly large selection of species but sometimes there is insufficient space for displaying the plants and no employees able to advise the customers or to care for the cacti properly.

The seven most important pieces of advice when buying cacti

Naturally, everyone wishes to purchase only the healthiest cactus specimens. As cacti are really quite tough, however, and will not show symptoms of neglect or disease for a long time, here are a few tips which should be observed when you go to buy cacti:

1. Check carefully whether the cactus is sitting firmly in its pot. It should be well rooted.

2. The most sensitive part of the whole cactus is the neck of the root. If it shows soft spots and discoloration, you can be sure that it is decaying from the inside out. You cannot always see this with the naked eye, so you might have to feel the neck of the root very carefully with your finger.

3. Do not accept any sick or pest-infested cacti (see the section on diseases, p. 29). Small white flakes of wool between the spines are an indication of mealy bug infestation. Sooty, black spots on the spines and epidermis are characteristic of an infestation of sooty mould. Grey to yellowish-brown, dry discoloration of a new shoot or base (not to be confused with cork formation at the base of the cactus) indicates an infestation of red spider mites, which are difficult to control and rapidly spread to other plants.

4. Do not choose any cacti which have been left standing for any length of time in dark, artificially lit corners. Light deficiency will encourage unhealthy, tall growth which, in turn, will weaken the plant and make it susceptible to disease and pests. These lanky cacti have unhealthy-looking shoots and are light green in colour, their spines look "starved" and the areoles are spaced too far apart.

5. Do not buy any cacti which start shooting or producing flowers before the proper time (see table, p. 16). Usually, this is brought about by raising the temperature and employing tricks with artificial lighting (instead of proper overwintering). The plants do not become ill through such treatment but will become more susceptible later on when you subject them to the correct overwintering system as appropriate to their species.

6. The general appearance of the body of the cactus may look rather different depending on the season of the year. Make sure to check that your chosen specimen has all the right characteristics at the time when you buy it (see table, p. 16).

7. Do not rush to buy a flowering cactus. Unlike other plants, you cannot automatically assume that a cactus is healthy merely because it is flowering. It can still flower even when suffering from reduced roots or decay, which is why you should check its state of health first! If it is healthy and flowering too, this should be a guarantee that, given the right care, it will probably flower every year.

Create an enchanted windowsill with small-growing and slow-growing cacti.

Tips on transporting

● A single cactus will usually be wrapped in paper for transporting it home. Nevertheless, make sure to hold the cactus by its pot when wrapping or unwrapping it as the spines may pierce the paper when you are handling it.

● If you are transporting several cacti, ask the shop for a small transport pallet made of poly-styrene, as used by traders. The cactus pots can be placed in the pre-moulded holes and the whole thing will then be transported simply

and easily without any accidents. An alternative: Stand the cactus pots in a small box or carton and fill the spaces with crumpled news-paper so that the pots cannot slide about during transport.

● During winter, cacti should be transported warmly wrapped up in a closed container. Make sure that your cacti are outside for only a very brief period. Cacti are very sensitive to cold, even the so-called "hardy" ones if they have become "soft" through cultivation and have not been grown to be genuinely hardy.

(From left to right, above)
Top row: *Rebutia muscula and vio-laciflora, Parodia chrysacanthion, Mammillaria zeilmanniana, hahniana, woodsii and carmenae, Gymnocalycium baldianum, Rebutia muscula, Parodia aureispina, Rebutia krainziana.*
Bottom row: *Brasilicactus hasel-bergii, Schlumbergera-hybrids (pink, red), Astrophytum myriostigma, Notocactus concinnus, Cleistocactus buchtienii, Gymnocalycium mihanovichii var. friedrichii and baldianum, Ferocactus recurvus.*

13

Dispatching cacti by post

Fashion a collar for the plant out of rolled up newspaper and wrap it around the neck of the root and the edge of the pot. The body of the cactus should be wrapped up in a thick layer of soft paper or foam rubber. Then tightly wrap the whole thing again in newspaper. Finally, pack it all in a suitable carton, filling out the spaces with crumpled paper or another material to absorb shocks.

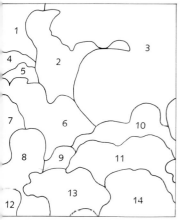

1. various Notocacti and Mammillaria
2. Cephalocereus senilis
3. Echinocactus grusonii
4. Notocactus werdermannianus
5. Mammillaria schiedeana
6. Mammillaria elegans
7. Mammillaria rhodantha
8. grafted cristates of Haageocereus
9. cristates of Mammillaria wildii
10. Mammillaria woodsii
11. cristates of Mammillaria geminispina
12. Mammillaria gracilis
13. cristates of Espostoa lanata
14. cristates of Echinofossulocactus

Danger of injury when handling cacti

Injuries from cactus spines can often be extremely painful. Although the spines are not toxic, injuries caused by them may allow dirt to enter the wound, which may then cause infection.

Important: If in doubt, be sure to consult a doctor about an injury.

How to avoid injuries

● Stand the cacti in such a way that unintentional contact with them is excluded from the start.

● Make sure they are kept out of reach of children and pets.

● If you have children or pets, you should, if possible, avoid keeping *Opuntia* (certainly *Cylindropuntia*). These are the "bad guys" among cacti. Their spines possess tiny, but very effective, barbs which are very painful to remove.

Further important tips

● If you touch the areole of an *Opuntia microdasys*, you will find your skin immediately pierced by scores of tiny spines. Most of these can be removed by carefully brushing them off the area of skin involved. The remainder will have to be removed with tweezers.

● *Mammillaria bocasana*, with its "fish-hooks" hidden away among delicate wool, has been a deathtrap for many an unwary mouse in a greenhouse. If you ever happen to get "hooked", do not pull back suddenly in fright! Gently move your finger or hand forward in the direction of the body of the plant and carefully unhook spine after spine from your skin, then gently take your hand away.

● The spines of *Cylindropuntia* are so sharp and strong that they can pierce the sole of a mountain boot. In some cases, their strong barbs may even necessitate a trip to the casualty unit of a hospital if they have penetrated deep into the skin. *Do not eat cacti*, even if they are

non-toxic. Some cacti contain alkaloids. The ingestion of *Lophophora williamsii* is damaging to human health as the plant contains the drug mescalin. If you consume parts of this plant, you might fall into a trance that could result in serious damage to your health.

Initial care at home

Once you have brought your newly acquired cacti home, make sure to provide them as far as possible with the conditions they are accustomed to in respect of position, light and almost constant temperature and you should have no transition problems with them.

Bright, but not intense, sunlight: Cacti under glass can only tolerate intense sunlight if they have always been accustomed to it. Temperatures can become so hot behind glass that the epidermis may burn. The first symptoms of this are soft, pale green, discoloured spots on the side facing the sun, which later turn brown and – providing the cactus survives – will eventually harden. If the cacti are placed in direct sunlight, they should be provided with shade until they have become accustomed to the conditions. Use plastic sheeting, greaseproof paper or paper painted with shading paint.

In winter: Keep them cool and do not water them. You will wish to make sure that the cactus does not start growing, so do not stand it in a place that is too warm and begin watering carefully in the spring.

In summer: water whenever necessary. If the new cactus has just begun to shoot or flower, treat it as described in the chapter on care (see p. 17).

How to tell whether cacti are healthy

	Epiphytes *Nopalxiochia, Phyllocactus, Rhipsalidopsis, Schlumbergera*	Cacti which display visible shrinkage and formation of folds during the winter dormancy period *Echinocereus, Opuntia*	Cacti which do not visibly shrink during winter dormancy *Astrophytum, Mammillaria, Notocactus, Parodia*
Winter	No new shoots, no shrinking; visible formation of buds in *Rhipsalidopsis*; flowering time of *Schlumbergera*.	Shrinkage and folding, no new shoots.	Hardly visible shrinkage; no growth; a dull appearance. Some *Neoporteria* will flower; some *Mammillaria* will form buds.
Spring	Beginning of new shoot formation and growth. Bud formation in *Phyllocactus*.	Beginning of new shoots and growth (the body begins to fill out) formation of buds and beginning of flowering.	
Summer	Fresh shoots on still-flowering *Phyllocacti*; late final flowering.	A full, strong body; fresh shoot formation; many cacti still in flower. If the heat is intense, cessation of growth may occur.	
Autumn	End of growth period, increasingly firm shoots (toughening up).	Preparation for dormancy: cessation of growth; shrinkage after watering ceases; formation of folds.	Cessation of growth; robust appearance; stragglers flower; bud formation in some *Neoporteria*.

Using artificial lighting in a position where there is insufficient natural light (see p. 24): You will only be able to tell if your cactus is not receiving enough light after some considerable time has passed: it will start growing tall rather quickly and, depending on the species, its spines will be less well developed. If it does not receive more light at this stage, it will form fewer or no flowers at all during the following year.

Stand sick cacti in an isolated position: If you have made the mistake of buying a sick cactus or one infested with pests – perhaps because it was a rarity or it appealed to you – it should be kept isolated from other plants and treated according to the time of year and the particular problem (see chapter on diseases, p. 19).

My tip: Be careful with propagators, balcony boxes and cold frames under direct sunlight! A lethal accumulation of heat can build up inside these if they are not properly ventilated!

How to care for an offset

It is a real pleasure to find oneself in charge of a tiny offset or "baby" cactus. This prickly little being should be carefully removed from the parent plant and given its own place in your plant collection. Very often it will not yet have formed roots, or perhaps just a few, but with correct care and attention it should soon grow some.

● Fill a small pot with cactus soil or a mixture of flower compost and sand and gently press in the offset.
● Do not water it for at least four to six weeks. This is how long it will take for the young cactus to form roots and "find its feet". Do not be afraid that it will die of thirst. Under certain conditions, it would be able to survive for a year or more without water or soil.
● Stand it in a bright, warm position, but not in full sunlight.
● When you can see the first root tips, water it carefully. A bright new shoot with fresh spines in the centre at the top is a sign of success.
● If the cactus was planted in a pot in winter, you will have to be patient. The spring sunshine will finally bring it back to life.

Care of cacti all year round

Successful cactus growing should result if you simply give these light-hungry desert plants what they require to live: the light they receive should duplicate the desert sun, the soil be like the ground in the desert, watering should imitate rain, fog and dew and fertilizing should replace the nutrients found in the wild. If all of these requirements are fulfilled, your prickly charges will flourish and turn into flowering beauties.

The optimal position

Stand your cactus in a place that will meet its requirements as closely as possible:

● plenty of light, sun and fresh air;
● warmth during the growth period (but avoid an accumulation of too much heat);
● cool temperatures and dryness during the dormancy period. From mid-autumn onwards, move the cactus to a cool (5-12°C/41-54°F) but bright position. Daylight hours will be decreasing at this time of year and the cactus will cease growing.

On a windowsill: Provide your cactus with a proper window seat (east-, south- or west-facing). North-facing windows do not provide enough light. If you stand the cactus on an outside window ledge, sheltered from rain, during the warm part of the year, you will be doing a great deal to promote its general well-being.

In a greenhouse: A heated greenhouse is the ideal position for cacti. During the winter, most cacti can cope with a cool greenhouse at temperatures below 10°C (50°F). For warmth-loving cacti, however (such as *Melocacti*), the temperature should not sink below 12°C

(54°F) for any length of time.

In a cold frame or balcony box: You may move cacti from their winter quarters to these positions from mid- to late spring onwards, but only leave them there until the autumn. The plants must be moved back to their winter quarters before the first frost.

Unsuitable positions

● Cacti are not suitable for display on a plant table indoors. They will not receive enough light in such a position.
● Cacti are not happy in a bathroom, as constant high humidity will kill them. If the temperature is persistently warm and there is plenty of fresh air, humidity will not be so harmful, but if temperatures are low, decay will set in.
● Badly insulated windows are anathema to cacti. Check during the winter to make sure your windows close properly, so that the plant is not allowed to get cold.

The right water

Cacti do not appear to react too sensitively to hard water (with a high content of lime), but lime may show up as a crusty, whitish-grey layer on the sides of the pot, on the surface of the soil and on the cactus. Apart

from creating an unattractive appearance, early repotting will become necessary.

You may measure the hardness of your water with chemical indicators (obtainable from shops specializing in laboratory supplies or equipment for aquariums), or find out the average degree of hardness of your water from your water authority or local council. If the average degree of hardness is over 13 degrees Clark, the water should be softened.

How to soften water for plants

● By adding solutions or powders (obtainable in the gardening trade).
● By using a filter (also available in the gardening trade).
● By using peat (without a fertilizer!) which is added to a pail of mains water in a ratio of 1 part peat to 3 parts water. Leave this to stand for one day. Strain off the peat before using the water.
● Aquarium owners may own an ion-exchange device. However, water that has been completely purified cannot be used and will have to be mixed with mains water again. The optimal degree of acidity is between 5 and 6.7 pH.

My tip: Rain water is soft but, depending on the locality, may contain various harmful substances to a greater or lesser extent. Use it only after filtering. If you intend to take it from a roof gutter, wait until after the first fall of rain.

When to water

Watering can often make the difference between life and death for a cactus. Most do not suffer from thirst but are watered to death instead. The quality of the water used is less important than the quantity and the time of watering.

The position, the surrounding temperature, the amount of sunlight, the soil, the material from which the pot is made, the general condition of the plant and the time of year are all deciding factors when it comes to how and when a cactus should be watered. Do not be discouraged, however, as cacti are robust plants and will not react violently to a few mistakes.

There are three basic rules for watering cacti. If you take them to heart, you will be able to care for your cacti properly.

1. It is better to water less often than too often – but when you do, do it thoroughly.

2. The cooler the position, the less water will be required.

3. The more humus the soil contains, the more carefully you should water as this soil will retain moisture longer than sandy, mineral soils. Another important point to remember when watering is to observe the seasonal rhythms of cacti.

In winter, during dormancy: Do not water if the cacti are kept in a cool position (below 10°C/50°F). Give very small quantities of water if the temperature is slightly warmer (above 10°C/50°F) and the weather is fine, but avoid starting up growth during the winter!

In spring, after the plant has begun to revive (that means, as soon as the first new spine appears at the top of the cactus or the first flowers open), water carefully. If the body of the cactus fills out after a few days and the plant begins to form new shoots, continue to water thoroughly! But water less during periods of colder, sunless weather.

From late spring to early autumn, during the main growth phase, water plentifully. In between, allow the soil to dry off well, and only then continue watering. Definitely avoid waterlogging.

NB: Plastic pots hold moisture for longer than clay pots! When the weather turns colder, delay watering and wait for warmer days. During very hot periods of weather, cacti kept under glass may temporarily cease growing altogether. If you notice this happening, you should stop watering immediately.

In the autumn, from about the middle of the season, stop watering. This is a signal to the cactus that its rest period is approaching.

How to water

If possible, water the cactus in such a way that the body does not become wet. If you want to give it a shower as part of the watering, use only clean water. Afterwards, stand it in fresh air where it will quickly dry off again. If the axil wool or woolly parts of flowers remain wet for lengthy periods of time, there is a great risk of decay.

Various methods of watering cacti

● Water along the gap between the cactus and the edge of the pot.
● Pour water into the dish underneath the pot.
● In the water storage method, the pots are set in larger vessels filled with water (or with a nutrient solution) so that the soil can absorb the water. Then remove the pot and allow it to drain off thoroughly. You can tell by the appearance of the surface of the soil if it is thoroughly soaked (use a finger to test it).

My tip: Make a point of avoiding waterlogging around the very sensitive neck of the roots. Bedding the neck of the roots in coarse, water-permeable soil will help more sensitive cacti to avoid decay.

Misting and spraying

Many cacti live in foggy deserts between a coast and high mountains. They utilize this high humidity as part of their water supply. By misting and spraying your cacti on hot summer and autumn evenings, you can provide them with this kind of precipitation. This procedure will also toughen them up in the autumn.

Points to note

● Only use water that is free of lime and at room temperature!
● Spray in such a way that no moisture remains on the body of the cactus (especially on the crown or in the axil wool)!

NB: Some cacti (like *Coryphantha* and *Ferocactus*) have glands on their areoles, which secrete a honey-like substance. Too much moisture (from spraying, too much watering or too much humidity) can cause a black mould to form on this secretion, which, although not harmful, is not very attractive.

Care while you are away

You can quite safely leave your cacti on their own during your absence. They will survive the ensuing dry period without coming to any harm. This is much better than leaving them to the tender mercies of a well-meaning but inexperienced neighbour, who might easily have watered them to death by the time you return. All you need to do is to water them thoroughly and fertilize them before your departure.

If you are growing cacti in a balcony box, cold frame or small greenhouse, you will need to provide sufficient ventilation during the summer months if you are going away and you must remember to turn on the heating in the winter! A reliable person to regulate the heating might be more important than someone to water the cacti while you are away.

A unusual beauty

Leuchtenbergia principis has long, tri-edged, frosty blue tubercles, with long, papery spines protruding in tangles from their ends (care, see p. 26).

What nutrients are required?

Like all other plants, cacti need nutrients. The normal supply of nutrients in a desert landscape is usually rather meagre, however, so cacti have adapted to this fact and have learned to make maximum use of what is on offer.

A cactus lives on the same basic elements as other plants: nitrogen, phosphorous and potassium. Nitrogen supports growth, phosphorous helps in the building of cells and the formation of flowers, and potassium is an all-round element needed for the well-being of the cactus and to boost its immune system to protect it against disease. In addition, a cactus will need minute quantities of trace elements. The main trace elements are magnesium, iron and manganese which aid the formation of chlorophyll. If these elements are lacking, the plant will turn yellow and suffer from chlorosis (lack of chlorophyll), which, in turn, will have a deleterious effect on photosynthesis.

The right kind of fertilizer

The ratio of the three main nutrients, nitrogen (N), phosphorous (P) and potassium (K) is usually indicated on the packaging of commercial fertilizers in the sequence N-P-K, 1:1:0.5 to 1:2:2. The important thing is that the content of nitrogen should be less or the same as the content of phosphorous. For this reason, fertilizers meant for flowering plants are better for cacti than fertilizers intended for foliage plants. Do not blindly trust the designation "cactus fertilizer". Check the consistency of nutrients and if they are not indicated on the packaging, do not buy the fertilizer.

The seven most important points about fertilizing

1. Always use the dose recommended by the manufacturer (or better, a slightly smaller dose).
2. Do not fertilize the cactus immediately after repotting it. The cactus will be able to derive the necessary nutrients from the fresh soil.
3. Never fertilize during the winter dormancy period.
4. Only start fertilizing during the growth phase, when the cactus displays a definite sign of new growth – so do not fertilize in the spring with the first watering!
5. Do not fertilize if the plant shows signs of damage to the roots!
6. Do not allow the fertilizer solution to run on to the plant (especially on the epidermis near the shoot tips). If necessary, rinse it off with clean water.
7. Before the cactus enters its well-earned winter sleep and you stop watering, give it a pure phosphorous fertilizer in the last lot of water. This fertilizer will promote the formation of flowers the following spring – always providing the cactus is capable of flowering!

My tip: Observe your cactus during its growth phase. It should grow vigorously but not unnaturally (see p. 29) and should not look bloated.

When to repot

Regular repotting will promote healthy growth even in cacti. As they make few demands on the nutrient content of the soil, however, this need not be done every year. Repot:
● as a rule every two to three years. Fast-growing and large-growing species may have grown over the edge of the pot before that time and will have to be repotted sooner. The best time of year is spring or early summer, if necessary even in the summer or early autumn, but the cactus should have time to recover before the onset of dormancy (mid-autumn);
● if the roots start appearing out of the drainage holes in the pot;
● if there are lime deposits around the pot, on the surface of the soil or on the lower parts or spines of the cactus;
● if the surface of the soil grows algae or moss;
● if the cactus does not continue growing even under favourable conditions;
● if there is a severe infestation of pests, particularly in the case of mealy bugs (see p. 31);
● in the case of tall-growing species (for example, *Cereus* species) the plant becomes top-heavy in its pot.

My tip: Never repot during the winter dormancy period. If it becomes necessary (for example, if the cactus shows signs of decay), remove the plant from its pot, clean the roots or remove them (see p. 22), allow the cut surfaces to dry off and leave the cactus to lie there – dry – until the following spring, when it can be repotted.

Clay or plastic pots?

Both of these types have their advantages and disadvantages.
A clay pot is porous and air- and water-permeable; the soil will dry out faster and will need watering more often. The nutrients are washed to the inside walls of the pot, so that the roots tend to grow towards the wall of the pot and no compact rootstock forms. Advantage: large plants are more stable in a clay pot.
A plastic pot allows the soil to dry out more slowly, which means that you need not water so often but must do so with more care. The nutrients are distributed more evenly in the soil, which promotes a more favourable development of the rootstock. Advantage: if you choose square plastic pots, you can accommodate far more cacti in a

Mammillaria, which are suitable for any windowsill, remain small, flower profusely and are very charming.

small space and will have a more compact area of cultivation.

My tip: The new pot should be a little wider in diameter than the body of the cactus, so that a space for watering remains. Cacti with turnip-like roots will fare better in taller pots. Columnar cacti will require a much larger pot, so that they obtain sufficient stability.

The right soil

Cacti grow in very different kinds of soil in their countries of origin. They are extremely flexible in cultivation, however, and will become used to many kinds of soil. The cactus grower's concern is not so much the choice of the right type of soil as caring properly for the cactus once it is planted in a given soil. *Humus-rich and nutrient-rich soils* are required by epiphytes (see p. 25), *Selenicereus* (see p. 57) and *Phyllocereus* (see p. 55).
Soils that are extremely water- and air-permeable are needed by cacti originating from desert and rocky terrains. These qualities are provided by mixtures consisting of coarse river gravel, pumice gravel, crushed lava, Perlite, crushed Hortag and only small amounts of humus or flower compost. Less-sensitive species can cope with larger amounts of added humus.
Purely mineral soils, like pumice gravel, lava-based gravel and mixtures containing quartz sand, broken brick fragments or wood charcoal granules, are required for sensitive or difficult cacti.

These cacti will have to be fertilized with great care.

Commercial cactus soil is very rich in humus and is made porous by the addition of sand and, sometimes, polystyrene flakes. This type of soil is not suitable for cacti species that originate from regular sand or gravel deserts, but it can be improved by adding sand and pumice gravel.

My tip: Pumice gravel is an ideal cactus soil. It keeps moist for longer and simultaneously ensures that the soil is well aerated. Water by the storage method (see p. 18). The pumice gravel will absorb water but will also allow surplus water to run away immediately and still retain a moisture reservoir for the cactus.

Handling cacti

Removing cacti from their pots and repotting them requires careful and knowledgeable handling.

● Have a good look at the cactus's spines before removing it from its pot. Some spines that are not too stiff can be made soft and pliable by moistening them. After that, you can touch them quite safely if wearing gloves or by using rags as pads.

● Really tough, stiff spines and spines with nasty barbs can be gripped in polystyrene (see illustration, right) or by a combination of gloves and paper. NB: when taking hold of the cactus, first grip it very gently then more firmly, so that you can tell the minute the spines threaten to penetrate the material.

● If you decide to get to grips with your cactus by using tongs (for example, kitchen tongs or even fire irons), you will have to use these with great care, especially in the case of soft-bodied cacti, if you do not wish to injure them.

● If you have already had some experience of handling cacti, you will know how and where to grip

them. Some species (for example, *Cleistocactus straussii*) can be handled quite safely by real cactus enthusiasts who stroke the spines and grip the cactus gently with their bare hands – without injuring themselves!

Tips when removing cacti from their pots

Make sure the rootstock is quite dry before you remove the cactus from its pot. This will make it much easier to extract the plant from the pot and will also avoid the risk of infection through roots being damaged while removing the plant.

Method: In the case of clay pots, very gently tapping the pot will loosen the rootstock and then a stick, inserted through the drainage hole, is used to push the rootstock out carefully.

In the case of plastic pots, gently squeeze and tap them so that the rootstock is loosened. Then, using a dibber or something similar, slide the cactus out of its pot (see illustration, below).

If the diameter of the pot is larger than the body of the cactus, hold the pot upside down and carefully tap the edge of it against the edge of a table. Place a dish underneath

it for the cactus to fall into (see illustration, below). If none of these methods works, the only thing left to do is to smash the pot or cut it up, respectively. Be cautious with plastic pots; the broken edges can be very sharp!

What to do before repotting

Now is the time to clean up the rootstock, which means removing old, dried up or decayed roots as well as the old, tired soil.

Old, decayed roots (they look shrunken, and the greyish-brown husk will fall off easily, leaving nothing but brown, tough fibres) and freshly decayed roots (dark brown, with damp patches) should be cut back to healthy tissue, which looks light and whitish.

Used soil should be removed. It will look hard and brittle and be full of calcium deposits, tend to smell stuffy or have a surface covered in moss or algae. A matted rootstock is also a sign of exhausted soil.

If the rootstock is completely healthy and the soil has not been exhausted, it will be sufficient just to brush over the surface of the rootstock with your hand.

Then, shake off the loose soil and the cactus is ready for repotting.

How to remove a cactus from its pot

1. If the diameter of the cactus is smaller than the edge of the pot, carefully tap the edge of the pot against the edge of a table and allow the cactus to fall into a dish. Do not touch it with your hands!
2. Plastic pots can be squeezed so that the rootstock is loosened, then push the cactus sideways out of the pot with the help of a dibber or knife.
3. Loosen the rootstock and grip the head of the cactus in polystyrene.

If there are signs of infestation by vine weevils, proceed as described on page 31. Do not repot the plant immediately, but allow the treated rootstock to lie in dry air for about one day.

How to repot

If the plant container and the soil (which should be quite dry) are all prepared and ready, you can go ahead.

● Cover the drainage hole of the pot with a pebble or a piece of broken pot.

● Fill the pot with soil (half to three-quarters full, depending on the size of the rootstock).

● Make a depression in the centre of the soil and plant the cactus at the same depth as it was before.

● Then, fill up the remainder of the pot with soil and gently press it down (perhaps with a dibber) between the rootstock and the edge of the pot.

● By gently tapping the pot on the table top or the ground, you will shake the soil down properly.

● Fill the pot with soil up to the edge of the pot, as it will sink down after the initial watering.

● In the case of more sensitive species of cacti, it is advisable to put a drainage layer of coarse soil at the bottom of the pot. In addition, it is a good idea to bed the neck of the roots in soil, in order to prevent waterlogging. This is particularly important if you are growing *Cephalocereus senilis*.

My tip: After repotting the cactus, do not water it for at least one week. Make sure that it is not placed in intense sunlight! Provide shade if necessary.

Cacti in hydroculture

Strictly speaking, hydroculture (hydroponics) means growing plants in water or in a nutrient solution.

Potting and repotting

1. Scrape some of the soil off the rootstock with a dibber and remove used up soil and decayed or dried up roots.
2. Cover the drainage hole, fill the pot with a drainage layer (broken pot shards or other coarse material), then fill the pot with soil.
3. Hold the cactus in the pot so that it is at the same level as in the previous one, then fill the pot all round with soil and press down well (use a dibber).

The plant is suspended in a vessel or medium with holes in it (for example, bedded in Hortag). The roots grow through this into a second, larger vessel which contains the nutrient solution. This type of culture is only suitable for cacti (for example, *Cereus* species) in exceptional cases. In a broader sense, one could look upon the culture of cacti in purely mineral soils (like pumice gravel, crushed lava, Perlite and so on) and then watering by the water storage method as hydroculture. For the rest, care is similar to care in other soils. At present, a large percentage of cacti are cared for in this way as even those cacti that are difficult to grow usually respond well to this method. The particular advantages are:

● A sudden large absorption of water and nutrients by the soil, which can quickly be utilized by the cactus.

● The soil and roots are well aerated, which leads to healthy root formation and prevents decay.

Overwintering

Not all cacti can be overwintered in the same way.

Cacti which originate from desert and mountainous regions like to be overwintered in bright, cool, dry surroundings. Only then will they produce beautiful flowers at the end of their dormant period.

● Optimal temperature: 5-12°C (41-54°F).

● The darker and cooler the position, the drier the cacti should be kept.

● If you are forced to let your cacti overwinter on a windowsill above a radiator, it will be necessary to water them occasionally (every three to four weeks). If possible, shield the plants from direct heat from the radiator by slipping a sheet of insulating material under the plants (for example, polystyrene).

● Many species (for example, *Lobivia, Rebutia* and *Notocacti*) can be overwintered in a dark place if there is no other solution, but the position must be completely dry and cool. Artificial light can serve well in dark positions (see p. 24).

● If a cactus begins to shoot during this period, it will grow lanky because of lack of light and will not flower in the spring.

Warmth-loving cacti (like *Melocacti* and *Discocacti*), on the other hand, really appreciate a sunny windowsill above a radiator as a place to overwinter.

Pelecyphora aselliformis – the "woodlouse cactus" from desert regions of central Mexico (care, see p. 26).

● The optimal overwintering temperature should be a constant 15-18°C (59-64°F).
● Water these cacti regularly but sparingly so that the soil never dries out completely.

My tip: Never fertilize cacti during the winter (except for epiphytes). The more they are left alone to enjoy their winter's sleep, the more gratefully they will flower in the spring.

Using electric light

If you are planning to grow your cacti exclusively under artificial light, you will be doomed to failure. They will never flower, as cacti only react to very high intensities of light.

My tip: Never place cacti under artificial light and then try to encourage them to shoot by providing warmth and extra watering. I can guarantee that they will then grow lanky and unhealthy, turn light green and produce long straggly extra growth along with extremely thin spines and widely spaced areoles.

Artificial lighting is fine if:
● you wish to extend daylight time on very dark days (especially in the autumn and winter) or if you want to provide more light;
● you are forced to overwinter cacti in a dark room (cellar or attic) when strong artificial light will activate photosynthesis and strengthen the plants' resistance. The following possibilities are available:

Ordinary light bulbs are not suitable, because they lack the blue range of the spectrum.

Fluorescent lights are cheapest but are also the weakest sources of light. They would have to be installed in large numbers at a distance of no more than 30 cm (12 in) from the cacti, in order to provide a sufficient intensity of light.

The cheaper commercial fluorescent light tubes with daylight-coloured light are more effective than the expensive special lamps with a higher degree of light in the red and blue ranges of the spectrum.

Mercury arc lamps and mixed light lamps can be obtained at very reasonable prices. They possess a very high intensity of light and their light spectrum is favourable for plants. They diffuse light in a cone shape, and the cacti should be placed with in this light. At a distance of 0.5 m (20 in), for example, a circle of light with a diameter of 0.7 m (28 in) is created. The closer the cacti are to the lamps, the better. If a larger area needs illuminating, it makes more sense to install several lamps, than to move the lamps further off.

Sodium arc lamps: The high output of light and the density of the rays, as well as the favourable spectral distribution of light, make them ideal plant lamps. Their purchase price, however, tends to be rather high as they can only be activited by a switching mechanism that has to be installed by an expert.

Epiphytes

Epiphytes are a special group within the realm of cacti, with their very own requirements in respect of care. They originate from warm, tropical areas where they flourish in humus "nests" in the forks of large trees. Epiphytes are leafy plants with short or long shoots and generally possess very few, inconspicuous spines which grow from areoles along the edges of the leaves or at the tips of their shoots.

Popular epiphytes
Marniera (see photo, p. 28);
Nopalxochia (see p. 52);
Phyllocactus (also *Epiphyllum*); (see photos, pp. 33 and 55);
Rhipsalis;
Rhipsalidopsis (Easter cactus) (see photo, p. 28);
Schlumbergera (Christmas cactus) (see p. 57);
Zygocactus (Christmas cactus) (see p. 57).

Caring for epiphytes

● They require humus-rich soil.
● They require less light than other cacti. The best site for them is a semi-shady position. Offer full sunlight only after the plant has become accustomed to lots of light and plenty of fresh air.
● From late spring to early autumn they will fare best outside in a position sheltered from the rain..
Phyllocactus (Epiphyllum),
in particular, is very suitable for growing on balconies or patios.
● Epiphytes do not like frost, nor a lot of heat.
● Indoors, they will be happy with a shady position, for example in a north-west-facing or north-east-facing window.
● Keep them slightly moist, never completely dry. During their growth period, they are very grateful for watering by the storage method (see p. 18).
● Fertilize them thoroughly during their growth and flowering period.
● When repotting, be generous with the size of the new pot, so that the cactus has plenty of good, nutrient-rich soil.

Overwintering epiphytes

Epiphytes are overwintered in different ways, depending on whether they belong to the group of winter-flowering or spring- and summer-flowering species.

Spring- and summer-flowering

species Nopalxochia, Phyllocactus, Rhipsalidopsis: do not let the soil dry out completely; temperature: 12-15°C (54-59°F); do not fertilize. *Selenicereus* should be overwintered in the same way (see p. 57).

Winter-flowering species
Marniera, Rhipsalis, Schlumbergera, Zygocactus: water well; temperature: around 20°C (68°F); fertilize sufficiently. If they are kept too dry, the flowers will drop off. After flowering, they will start growing again as early as winter right into the spring when new leaves will start forming. Wait until the end of spring before taking the plants outdoors. There, the young shoots will toughen up before autumn and, later on, will form flowerbuds again.

Cactus groups in bowls

The optimal grouping consists of low-growing cacti and those that stay spherical, planted in staggered formations of increasing height and – depending on the size of the bowl – including one or two decorative column-shaped cacti (for example, *Cleistocactus straussii*, *Cephalocereus senilis* or a *Espostoa*) as a background.

Cacti should be arranged according to their size. Stand the bowl in such a way that the small ones are at the front nearest the light and are not in the shadow of the larger ones.

Only combine cacti with similar requirements for care, so that conditions and the type of soil will be the same for all of them. For this reason, epiphytes or climbing cacti (like "Queen of the Night") are not suitable for such combinations. Care will be similar to that of cacti in individual pots. Exception: Water less but more often. This will prevent stagnant waterlogging at the bottom of the bowl.

Be careful with fast-growing cacti! Do not combine *Cereus* species and *Trichocereus* species with species that remain small. Fast-growing species will soon require larger, deeper containers.

Watch the direction of the light! Position the bowl in such a way that the smaller cacti are at the front, nearer to the source of light.

My tip: Make sure to take into consideration the growth tendencies of the various species. Some grow tall, others grow wider or form groups.

Cacti as large container plants

Large-growing cacti species, like *Cereus, Trichocereus, Opuntia* or *Echinocactus grusonii, Echinopsis* species and *Phyllocacti* (*Epiphyllum* hybrids) are all suitable as large container plants. Choose a position that will not permit injury to children or pets.

Caring for cacti in large containers
● The position should be sheltered from rain.
● Overwintering (see p. 23).
NB: Do not bring the plants into cool winter quarters until the soil has completely dried.
● In spring, take time to get the plants used to sunlight.

Cacti in greenhouses

If you create the right conditions, you can care for all cacti in the best possible way in a greenhouse. The most important point is cover.

Modern materials like double plates of plexiglass or something similar are ideal because they let in a lot of light and still insulate well and keep the plants warm.

Very important: good ventilation near the top of the greenhouse under the roof, in order to prevent accumulation of heat and burning of the plants.

The basic arrangement consists of 1 m (40 in) high shelves which can accommodate the plant pots.

How to care for cacti in a greenhouse
● Place the warmth-loving and less-sensitive cacti on the side of the greenhouse that is most exposed to sunlight.
● Square pots and dishes make best use of the available space on the shelves.
● It is advisable to place clay pots in peat or peat-sand mixtures as the soil tends to dry out quickly under intense exposure to sunlight.
● Watering and fertilizing should be as in other positions.
NB: Make sure the area is well ventilated! A high degree of humidity will promote growth but will also encourage the formation of fungi, moulds and decay.
● Spraying and airing the plants in the evenings will help to toughen them up in the autumn. Warning: do not spray if there is any risk of night frosts.
● If warmth-loving cacti and those that prefer cool temperatures are overwintered together, place the warmth-loving ones in positions nearer to a radiator or some similar source of heat.

My tip: Stand the cactus pots in flat dishes, then they can be watered quite easily by the storage method in summer (see p. 18). Once the soil has absorbed enough moisture, make sure to remove any surplus water.

Cacti for your greenhouse

Ariocarpus kotschoubeyanus (photo. p. 27)
Flowers in the autumn, has a turnip-like root.
Care: very sunny position, mineral soil, carefully
dosed watering, grows on its own rootstock.
Overwintering: cool, dry.

Aztekium ritteri (photo, p. 27)
Vigorously shooting dwarf cactus.
Care: warm, no intense sunlight, mineral soil,
grow as a grafted plant.
Overwintering: cool, dry.

Heliocereus speciosus (photo, p. 39)
Epiphyte-like, large container plant.
Care: semi-shade, nutrient-rich, slightly humus-containing soil, water well, grows on its own rootstock.
Overwintering: 12-15°C (54-59°F), slightly moist.

Leuchtenbergia principis (photo, p. 19)
"Prism cactus", turnip-like root.
Care: very sunny position, mineral soil, grows on its own rootstock.
Overwintering: plenty of light, cool and dry.

Mamillopsis senilis (photo, p. 3)
Forms attractive clumps.
Care: strong sunlight, mineral soil, grow it on its own rootstock.
Overwintering: very cool, dry.

Pelecyphora aselliformis (photo, p. 24)
A shoot-forming dwarf cactus with comb-like arrangements of spines.
Care: sunny, mineral soil, grow it on its own rootstock.
Overwintering: cool, dry.

Cacti in large beds

In large greenhouses you will have an ideal opportunity to plant out cacti in large beds.

Usually, the bed will be situated in the centre of the greenhouse. If not, the greenhouse should be insulated along the outside wall and along the floor with polystyrene sheets. The bed should be bordered with a thin wall of concrete or bricks and the installation of floor heating that can be regulated would be ideal.

● Depth of the bed: 40-60 cm (16-24 in). If this is not possible, 20 cm (8 in) will do.

● Use good, water-permeable soil.

● Choose cacti with almost identical requirements for care, for example, no epiphytes.

● Leave some room between the cacti as they will grow large quicker in a bed than in pots. Even if the freshly planted bed looks a little sparse and empty, in two or three years' time the picture will be quite different.

● Plant the cacti directly into the soil, not in pots sunk into the soil, as they will root very quickly and then, if you want to take them out again, they could be injured very easily.

● Avoid using small-growing cacti as they will look quite lost in a large bed.

Cacti recommended for large beds

For a background: nearly all *Cerea, Cleistocactus, Espostoa, Myrtillocactus, Oreocereus, Trichocereus.*
For the middleground: *Cephalocereus, Echinocactus, Echinocereus, Echinopsis, Ferocactus, Haageocereus,* larger *Lobivia, Notocacti* and *Mammillaria.*
For the foreground: *Dolichothele, Echinocereae, Lobivia,* smaller *Mammillaria, Notocactus* and *Parodia.*

Aztekium ritteri is reminiscent of Aztec art (care, see p. 26).

Ariocarpus kotschoubeyanus from central Mexico (care, see p. 16).

Cactus flowers

The lifespan of a cactus flower is very short and some of them open only at night. However, they are treasured by all who see them because of their cheerful colours and will continue to produce new flowers during the flowering phase.

1. Echinocereus triglochidiatus with its typically green stigma – a hardy cactus (care, see p. 45).
2. Austrocactus patagonicus will became hardy after it has become acclimatized but is difficult to care for.
3. Lobivia backebergiana – fiery colours from the highest mountains of the Cordilleras ranges (care, see p. 49).
4. Sulcorebutia rauschii, a dwarf from the Bolivian highlands (care, see p. 58).
5. Notocactus roseoluteus, a pink-yellow-flowering meadow dweller from Argentina (care, see p. 53).

6. The giant flowers of Marniera chrysocardium (an epiphyte), which can also be planted in hanging baskets. In the foreground is the star-shaped stigma (care, as for epiphytes, see p. 25).
7. Rhipsalidopsis gaertneri, "Easter cactus" (epiphyte) displays its beautiful star-shaped flowers around Easter time (care, see p. 25).
8. Echinocereus pectinatus var. rubispinus rolls back its petals in great heat (care, see p. 45).
9. Echinocereus longisetus has to be watered particularly carefully (care, see p. 45).

Pests and diseases

It is well known that cacti are fairly resistant to illness and seldom fall victim to pests and diseases – they are far more likely to suffer from incorrect overfeeding or watering. The right care is the best prevention against disease as it does not allow diseases a chance to take hold. If pests and diseases do still occur, however, you will need to know how to get rid of them.

Prevention

Optimal care is the be-all and end-all in maintaining your cacti's resistance.

● Keep strictly to the correct growth periods.

● Toughen up your plants with plenty of fresh air.

● Observe the strictest hygiene when repotting a plant (clean pots, fresh soil), grafting (clean implements) and on all other occasions when you have to cut the cactus in any way, so that no harmful bacteria can enter the plant.

● Make sure conditions that promote decay are avoided (this is usually the result of infestation by fungi). Supply fresh air and good hygiene, regularly allow the soil to dry properly before watering again and avoid lengthy periods of high humidity.

● Unattractive developments, which are not diseases, like splits caused by stress (see p. 30) or cork formation (see p. 30), will be prevented by proper care.

Plant protection agents

Once you have identified the particular pest or disease that is affecting your plants, you can seek out the correct plant protection agent to use against this. The best thing to do is to consult a good local garden centre or specialist nursery as to what preparation to use. You must definitely take advice from specialists if the preparation you intend to use is toxic and must also follow the manufacturer's instructions to the letter. In the gardening trade, all toxic products are kept under lock and key and will only be handed out by specially trained employees. Use chemical sprays with the greatest caution. If at all possible, use biological (organic) agents.

Warning: All plant protection agents, even biological ones, must be stored in a place that is inaccessible to children and pets. Only use sprays outside!

Alternative forms of control

More and more products appear for sale these days, many of them intended to protect plants through biological methods. Here again, you should seek advice from trained personnel at your local garden centre. Experienced cactus enthusiasts, cactus raisers and local or national cactus societies will also be glad to help you.

Reluctance to bloom

Symptoms: the cacti refuse to flower, even if they have bloomed before.

Causes: mistakes in care, lack of rest in winter (too warm, too moist, too dark); nitrogen-rich and phosphorous-poor fertilizing.

Remedy: proper overwintering (see p. 23) and fertilizing (see p. 20).

Cessation of growth and shrinkage

Symptoms: sudden cessation of growth during the growth period, in spite of proper care, shrinking of the body of the cactus.

Causes: mistakes in care, decayed roots or roots infested with vine weevils.

Remedy: repot (remove old soil and decayed roots, cut back to the healthy, light-coloured roots), or see vine weevils (p. 31).

Unnatural or extreme growth

Symptoms: bloated body, shiny epidermis, new shoots are thin, pointed and light green and the spines are not properly formed.

Causes: mistakes in care, too much heat, over-fertilizing (too much nitrogen) coupled with lack of light

Remedy: stop fertilizing, reduce watering, slowly provide more light.

Yellow discoloration

Symptoms: the epidermis becomes yellow and increasingly pale.

Causes: mistakes in care; magnesium, iron and manganese deficiencies (chlorosis).

Remedy: use a special fertilizer and repot the plant in nutrient-richer soil.

Damage from burns
Symptoms: first, red discoloration, then parts of the body become first soft, spongy and whitish-brown, then hard after several days.
Causes: mistakes in care, too sudden and intense exposure to sunlight, accumulation of heat.
Remedy: only prevention is possible; provide shade until the plant has become accustomed to the sun and fresh air.

Aphids
Symptoms: only occur on epiphytes (on fresh, delicate shoots, buds and flowers).
Causes: draughts, infestation from other plants.
Remedy: remove them by hand or spray the plant with insecticide.

Nematodes
Minute worms which infest the roots and cause the formation of knots and cysts among them.
Symptoms: weaker growth, which may end in the plant dying through lack of nutrition.
Causes: infestation from other plants.
Remedy: radically cut back the roots, if necessary, even the neck of the roots, then treat the cactus like a cutting (see p. 35). Remove the pot, the soil and the roots that were cut off and destroy them!

Bacterial diseases
These do not occur very often.
Symptoms: the plant tissues turn dark green, spongy and slimy and then disintegrate.
Causes: infection from infested soil, water or other sick plants.
Remedy: prevention with strict hygiene and a sunny overwintering position. Cut back the infected parts to the healthy tissue, disinfect the wound, allow to dry.

Viral diseases
These do not occur very often.
Symptoms: altered growth, in the case of *Opuntia* broom-like growth through overproduction of shoots; other cacti display cauliflower-like growths.
Causes: infestation by insects that suck the plants' juices.
Remedy: cut out the unnatural growths, allow the wound to dry well, disinfect with charcoal powder; usually the cactus will return to normal.

Root decay
Symptoms: missing shoots in the growth period; often the cactus can be lifted off the soil without any resistance.
Causes: generally infestation with fungi (or other causes, like waterlogging).
Remedy: cut back the decayed roots; completely renew the soil. Disinfect the pots before reusing them. If necessary, treat the cactus like a cutting (see p. 35).

Wet and soft decay
The most serious fungal diseases!
Symptoms: decay which rises upwards from the neck of the roots towards the tips of the new shoots. The colour of the decay is watery olive green to pale brown and may appear in spots on the epidermis.
Remedy: the plant can only be saved if the condition is recognized in its very early stages. Cut back the tissue to where the ring of vascular tissue shows no brown or yellowish colouring and is a healthy white. Dust the surface of the wound with charcoal powder or a chemical fungicide. Allow the cactus to dry in the air. Then prepare it for rooting.
NB: Disinfect all tools and implements with alcohol, particularly before cutting into the cactus tissue.

Splits caused by stress
Symptoms: the epidermis develops a tear along the side of the body of the cactus. This often happens in the case of grafted cacti (especially *Gymnocalycium, Lophophora* and *Turbinicarpus*)
Cause: too rapid growth.
Remedy: reduce growth by watering and fertilizing less. Allow the wound to dry out in fresh air.

Cork formation
Symptom: formation of cork-like, brown epidermis from below (typical for *Notocacti*).
Cause: often a sign of old age.
Remedy: not possible but with correct care the cactus will carry on growing healthily, so that the visually unattractive cork formation is not that noticeable.

Fungal infection of seedlings
Symptoms: seedlings and soil are covered in a whitish fluff, the seedlings turn dark green, look bloated and watery, then disintegrate. *Cause:* fungal infection. *Remedy:* prevention: observation of strictest hygiene during sowing (see p. 34). Remove affected parts and soil, spray the rest with a fungicide or water and provide plenty of fresh air.

Mealy bugs
Symptoms: white woolly cocoons in the axils, on the inner edges of the ribs or in the folds of the neck of the roots. The bugs are whitish to reddish and look like woodlice. *Cause:* infestation from other cacti or invasion by adult bugs. *Remedy:* remove the insects with a small brush. Spray with an insecticide and only water during the growing period.

Red spider mites
Symptoms: the most dangerous pest, especially for soft-bodied cacti. Pale epidermis, tiny yellowish-brown spots which enlarge to form patches, starting at the shoot tips. *Cause:* transmission from other plants or via draughts. *Remedy:* spray with an insecticide, employ useful predatory insects or, if severe, destroy the cactus.

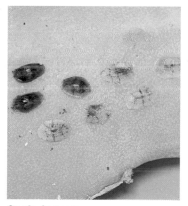

Sun damage
Symptom: discoloration of the epidermis – red, later yellow, on the side facing the sun. *Cause:* mistakes in care, the cactus develops a protective pigment called anthocyan. *Remedy:* shade and plenty of fresh air. The discoloration may fade. *NB:* If it does not, there may be damage to the roots.

Scale insects
Symptoms: light to dark brown "caps" which serve as a hiding place for the insects. The young move about and secrete a sticky substance. *Cause:* transmission from other plants. *Remedy:* it is a fairly rare condition, so it is possible to scratch them off. If infestation is severe, spray with a suitable agent.

Vine weevils
Symptoms: cessation of growth, red colouring, persistent shrinkage. Powdery white nests in the rootstock and roots. *Causes:* infected soil, transmission from other plants. *Remedy:* remove the soil and clean the roots. Repot and, after two weeks, water with an insecticide and repeat several times.

Propagating and grafting

There can hardly be another plant whose propagation is so simple and so fascinating. Whether you are raising a new hybrid or propagating particularly beautiful cacti for yourself or friends from cuttings or shoots, you will be surprised how easily you will succeed. As many cacti adapt well to each other, you can also propagate by grafting.

Propagating from seed

Growing cacti from seed is by no means a long, tedious procedure as some people seem to believe. Many seedlings will flower after only two or three years. You can obtain cactus seed in garden centres and nurseries which sell selections of seeds of mixed genera and species of cacti.

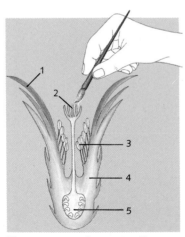

The structure of a cactus flower
1. petals; 2. style and stigma;
3. stamens; 4. tube with scales;
5. ovary.

If you want to grow particular species, it is better to turn to a specialist cacti nursery or seed supplier. Your local garden centre should be able to supply an address or catalogue for one of these. You may also obtain seeds from a local or national cactus society or from other cactus growers.
An alternative is to produce your own seeds! There can be no seeds without pollination, however, which means that you will have to work with flowering cacti. Transfer the pollen from one plant on to the stigma of another (illustration left). There are a few cacti which auto-pollinate, that is, they pollinate themselves, but most of them are sterile to their own pollen and still require a partner. Of course, you will only obtain pure species if you use two plants of the same species. If pollination occurs between different species or genera, hybrids are created – which can be either exciting or disappointing in appearance. Cacti seeds are usually ripe by autumn and ready to be sown.

My tip: Do not be disheartened if you want to obtain offspring of cacti that have flowers which bloom at different times. Cut off a few sta-

mens with anthers from the earlier-flowering cactus. Wrap them carefully in tissue paper and store them in your fridge. As soon as the "partner" plant opens its flowers, pollinate the stigma with the cooled pollen. It does work!

When to sow

Do not store harvested seeds too long, as their ability to germinate will decrease with time. The best results will be achieved with freshly harvested seeds.
The best time to sow seed is during the months from late winter to mid-spring. The seedlings will then be growing within the main growth period of cacti and, by the autumn, just before the winter dormancy period, they will have turned into strong, healthy little plants. If you wish, however, you can leave sowing until early autumn but in this case you will have to look after the seedlings well during the winter (heating, artificial light), so that they do not go into dormancy.
Other sowing times are not recommended because they go against the natural growth rhythms of cacti.

Successful sowing

Do not start without the right utensils.
You will need:
● a seed dish with a transparent plastic cover (or polythene sheeting or plate of glass);

Phyllocactus hybrid – a large container plant which flowers profusely and decoratively and is particularly suitable for balconies and patios. Easy to propagate from leaf cuttings

- square plastic pots which are placed in the dish;
- a bright, warm windowsill or a heating pad. Heatable mini-propagators (obtainable in the gardening trade) are ideal for windowsills;
- the soil should be fine-grained, poor in humus and, if possible, germ-free. The best kind is a mixture of fine pumice gravel, coarse quartz sand and a very little fine peat. Bake the soil in an oven for two hours at about 170°C (338°F) to destroy all bacteria and fungus spores, then allow it to lie for one or two days before use.

Treatment of seeds before sowing

Harmful fungus spores and matter which decays easily are very often attached to cactus seeds, so they should be disinfected before sowing. Prepare a potassium permanganate solution (1 knife tip to ¼ litre/½ pt water) and put the seeds in it. Stir, then pour the solution through a paper coffee filter and lay the seeds on kitchen paper to dry. *NB:* Some seeds will be too small for this procedure.

How to sow

- Fill the seed pots with soil.
- Very small seeds should be sprinkled on to the soil (distribute well). Larger seeds should be lightly covered with soil so that they come into contact with the moisture in the soil.
- Make sure the seeds are separated according to species in their seed pots and remember to stick a label on the pot with the name of the species etc. written on it.
- Stand the seed pots in the dish or tray and water them from below (*never* from the top). Use warm, soft water (softening water, see p. 17). The soil is thoroughly soaked if the surface looks shiny and dark.
- Remove surplus water.
- Place the seed tray on a warm base on a very bright windowsill.

Pricking out seedlings

1. *Loosen the seedlings then lift each seedling out of the seed pot with a piece of paper (or very carefully with your fingers).*
2. *Make a hole in the fresh soil in the prepared tray with a thin stick.*
3. *Set the seedling in the soil and press the soil down well with a stick.*

- The ideal germinating temperature is 28°C (82°F). A thermostat with a control is a great help.

Development and growth of the seedlings

The first two seedling leaves will sprout after two or three days. Most of the seeds, apart from a few stragglers, will have germinated after ten to twelve days. Only a few species (for example, *Opuntia*) take longer to germinate (four to six weeks). After two to three weeks the body of the cactus seedling appears in the depression between the first two tiny leaves and will start forming its first spines, which look like fine, tiny hairs.

Care during the first two to three weeks:

Keep the soil warm and moist. Protect the seedlings from too much intense sunlight – shade them (for example, with tissue paper) and allow fresh, but not cold air into the propagator (open the lid a little). If temperatures rise above 35°C (95°F), the ability to germinate will decline rapidly.

Care to the pricking out stage:

As soon as the tiny shoots are visible between the germling leaves, allow plenty of light and fresh air to reach the little plants and continue to keep the soil warm. Allow the surface of the soil to dry occasionally; this will prevent the formation of mould or fungi and also stop algae forming. At this stage you can remove the cover or lid during the day as long as room temperatures are maintained.

Pricking out: As soon as the seedlings begin to "jostle" each other, it is time to prick them out.

- Ideal plant containers are small plastic or polystyrene dishes.
- Cover the drainage holes and fill the pots to just below the edge with fresh, fine-grained, slightly moist soil.
- Before removing the seedlings from the seed pots, loosen the old soil (by running a knife down around the edge of the pot) to prevent the roots from being damaged.
- How to transplant the seedlings is shown in detail in the illustration above.
- Stand the tray of transplanted seedlings in a bright, warm position, but protect them from intense sunlight.
- The freshly pricked out seedlings should be carefully watered one week after transplanting at the very earliest.

Do not water properly until there is evidence of real growth. However, the soil should never become completely dry all the way through, otherwise the fine fibrous roots would dry up.

● Leave the seedlings in this tray until they begin to crowd each other. Now they can be planted in deeper dishes or in suitable pots.
● The young cacti can now be cared for just like large cacti.

Problems with sowing

Seedling fungus appears fairly often (see p. 31). Prevention is achieved by disinfecting the soil and seeds before sowing. If the fungus still occurs, treat the seeds with a solution of fungicide (ask at your garden centre etc.) or dust them with a commercial fungicide powder. Give them plenty of fresh air!

Avoid decay by removing the empty seed husks and any seeds that have not germinated.

Sciarid flies often infest seedlings. Their tiny, maggot-like larvae eat the roots and root necks of delicate seedlings. Use a plant protection agent to treat the infested seedlings. This fly can also be controlled with bio friendly greenhouse fly catcher strips or special sticky yellow cards.

Propagating from offsets

While growing new cacti from seed will always produce descendants which share characteristics of both the mother and father plants, offsets and cuttings will always have the same genetic material as the parent plant. If the parent plant has already produced flowers, you will find this method of propagation to be the fastest and surest way of obtaining large cacti that are able to produce flowers.

My tip: If a cactus from which you would like to propagate offspring does not produce offsets, cut a piece of it off at a visually suitable place. Then treat this piece just like a cutting (above right) or a grafted cactus (see p. 36) and allow the wound surface on the parent plant

to dry off in the air. The cactus will usually form offsets along the top areoles and these can then be removed for propagating purposes.

Method

The best time to take offsets is early spring to early autumn. Using a clean knife, a razor blade or a small pair of scissors, carefully separate an offset from the main body of the cactus. In the case of large cacti, take offsets when they are as young as possible as they will root more easily than older offsets. Treat the wound surface of the offset with rooting powder or dust it with charcoal powder, but it is sufficient to allow the cut surface of the parent plant to dry in the air.

Then stand the offset in a container with the cut surface up. The diameter of the top of the container should be smaller than that of the offset, so that air can circulate around the dried wound of the offset.

Position: warm, bright (no intense sunlight) and airy.

Light misting in the mornings and evenings will be good for the offset. After a few weeks, the first root tips will appear from the ring of vascular tissue, where the offset was cut. Now, place the offset, roots down, on top of slightly moist soil in its future pot. As soon as it has rooted well, slowly accustom it to sunlight and then care for it as you would for other cacti.

Propagating from cuttings

Cuttings are pieces of shoots cut from the parent plant or from its offsets. A cutting can be taken:
● when the mother plant is too old, too large or has become unattractive around the base (see cork formation, p. 30);
● to improve the appearance of a shoot that has grown too long;
● if you want to salvage the healthy head of a sick plant.

Method

Cut the cactus at a place that is visually favourable (for example, at a narrow place) or one that results from cutting back a sick plant.

In the case of old cacti, take the top part which is made up of younger tissue. This will root more quickly and surely.

If you want to continue using the lower part of the cactus, allow the cut surface to dry thoroughly. In time, offsets will grow from the surface. Care for this as usual. Trim the cutting on all sides to create a wedge shape (see illustration, p. 36) so that the vascular tissue is longer than the surrounding epidermis and tissue. Given the proper care, roots will grow out of the ring of vascular tissue.

Just like an offset, the cutting should be dried off well so that a protective skin can form over the wound. It may be treated with hormone powder or charcoal powder. Now stand it in an airy place, with the dried surface downwards, and mist it regularly.

As soon as the first roots show, set the cutting on slightly moist soil.

Grafting

This method involves fusing part of one plant (scion) to the cut surface of a robust, fast-growing second one (stock). The stock supplies the scion with nutrients just as if it were its own shoot. The choice of the right stock plant will determine the success of the method (see table, p. 37). Not all cacti will provide good stocks for grafting. The stock and the scion must definitely be compatible with respect to their growth period and requirements for care. Badly chosen stocks may sometimes reject the scion or cause it to take on an appearance that is completely unlike the scion's species.

Removing grafted cacti: Grafted cacti can be removed from their stock later on and then rooted without problems. This is a particular advantage in seedling grafting, for example, when the desired size of the grafted plant (perhaps around flowering age) has been attained.

Tips on grafting

Grafting will only be successful if the stock and the scion touch all across the joint surfaces of the ring of vascular tissue. This is the only place where they will be able to

grow together. Nutrients are transported across the joins of the vessels in the ring of vascular tissue. If the rings are of different sizes, the scion will have to be grafted on to the base in such a way that crossovers, or touching points, are created from one ring to the other. If this does not happen, the graft will not grow.

The ideal grafting season is when the stock is shooting, from mid-spring to early autumn, in warm weather. If you are forced to do an emergency grafting outside this period, the stock should have been prepared to start it shooting some weeks before grafting.

Make sure you have various kinds of support at hand, for example, wide rubber bands or support sticks with padding. Cut off the scion below the appointed place, using a sharp knife or razor blade. Trim around it slightly to form a wedge (see illustration below) and remove any spines that get in the way. As the cut surfaces will shrink inward when drying, cutting it in a wedge shape will prevent the scion and stock from touching only along the epidermis.

Stock: Make the cut towards the top of the plant if possible, where

fresh shoots are growing. Fresh tissue is more willing to grow. If the diameter of the ring of vascular tissue is much smaller than that of the scion, cut it across again, further down. Now trim the base to form a truncated cone (see illustration below).

Grafting on the scion: Before bringing the scion and stock together, cut off a thin slice of each so that the cut surfaces are completely fresh and moist. Then, using gentle pressure (do not squash the tissues!), place the scion on the stock. Make sure the rings of vascular tissue of each side meet and cover or at least touch or overlap.

How to tie them: Use rubber bands to secure the scion to the pot (see illustration below) or tie it to the spines of the stock so that it will not move.

Care after grafting

Stand the grafted plants in a warm, bright position. Shelter them from intense sunlight and keep the soil slightly moist.

If the grafting is a success, the two plants will have fused together after a few weeks. The body of the scion will fill out and begin to shoot. The rubber bands or other devices can now be removed. Further care (watering and fertilizing) should be given as appropriate to the requirements of the stock plant as it is the roots of the stock plant that are in the soil.

If the graft is unsuccessful, the scion will look limp and can be removed quite easily from the stock. Try cutting the stock and the scion again or, better still, choose a new stock.

Grafting

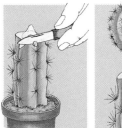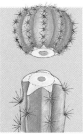

1. Find a healthy, growing stock. Cut through the new tissue below the tip of the shoot. Chamfer the cut surface conically.
2. Cut off a scion and again chamfer the edge of the cut surface.
3. Cut another thin slice off the stock and scion and place the cut surfaces together so that the rings of vascular tissue are in contact. Secure with rubber bands.

Well-tried grafting stocks

Echinopsis (all species)
For all low-growing scions; for slow-growing or rare *Echinocereus* types; for *Sclerocacti*, *Pediocacti* and *Utahia*; for cactus scions that like cool overwintering.
NB: will shoot vigorously; remove offsets regularly.

Eriocereus jusbertii
For warmer, slightly moist positions and overwintering; good as a permanent stock; young plants provide good stocks for seedling grafting.

Hylocereus hybrids
Vigorously shooting, epiphyte stock for warmer, slightly moist positions and overwintering; good for seedling grafting but not as a permanent stock.

Peireskiopsis
For warmer, slightly moist positions and overwintering; for scions which remain small; for seedling grafting but not as a permanent stock.

Selenicereus
Species: *Selenicereus grandiflorus*, *Selenicereus macdonaldiae*.
For warm overwintering; for shaping a Christmas cactus (*Schlumbergera* as a scion); for seedling grafting.

Trichocereus
Species: *Trichocereus pachanoi*, *Trichocereus spachianus* and others. For dry, cool overwintering; for growing scions to a certain size (on large stocks, up to four times the original size).
NB: *Trichocereus spachianus* shoots vigorously, so remove offsets regularly.

Variation 1: seedling grafting
This is a method for quickly obtaining larger cacti that are ready to flower. It is also good for growing species that are difficult or rare.
Scion: Cut off a seedling that is several weeks old and already displays a few spines. The vascular ring is still tiny and undeveloped.
The stock must be very young and cut off just below the tip of the shoot.
Alternative: If the stock is meant to "push" the seedling on, choose a robust-looking stock with a well-defined vascular ring. Set the seedling on a main vein of the vascular ring belonging to the stock. You can even accommodate several

seedlings on one broad ring – leave spaces so that the seedlings have room to grow.
Grafting: Set the seedlings on to the stock very gently, for example by first sticking them to the sticky surface of a paper label that is also attached to a knitting needle standing upright in the soil.
NB: Seedlings should be removed later on so that they can form their own roots, or for grafting them on to a permanent stock.

Variation 2: reverse grafting
With this type of grafting, a single cactus, that is difficult to grow on its own rootstock, can be propagated several times over.
Using the head as a scion: Cut the cactus in half across the middle and use the head as a scion.
Use the bottom part as a stock: Cut notches in the edge, sloping slightly downwards. Then, cut the roots off at the neck. Turn the cactus upside down, with the neck upwards. Set the notched surface on a robust stock so that there is contact between the vascular rings of both plants.
NB: If the grafting is successful, it will not take long before the "reversed" original part grows new offsets which, in turn, can be propagated again.

Variation 3: emergency grafting
This method is useful for saving cacti which have decayed from the neck upwards.
Scion: Cut away the upperparts of the cactus until the vascular ring looks white and the cell tissue looks fresh and a juicy greenish-white, without any brown veins.
The stock should be robust and shooting.

Variation 4: grafting to preserve non-viable cacti
Chlorophyll-free cacti, for example, *Gymnocalycium mihanovichii var. friedrichii* (see photo, p. 13) and *Chamaecereus silvestrii* cannot stay alive by themselves. If they are grafted on to a growing stock (usually *Hylocereus* or *Eriocereus*), they can obtain the plant surface that is vital for photosynthesis and this will keep the scions alive.

Popular cacti – care and advice

It is easy to be seduced by the glowing colours of the flowers and the infinite and fascinating shapes of the cactus family. Below is a selection of the most popular genera which will flower and flourish on most windowsills. The spectacular colour photographs, descriptions, special tips on care and recommendations for certain species will give you lots of ideas and make caring for cacti a real pleasure.

All the splendid specimens shown here were raised by plant growers and are available in the specialist trade. It really is not necessary to rob the natural world of wild cacti. Cacti that were raised to a state of unblemished beauty under nursery supervision beneath the bright sun of Teneriffe, Gran Canaria or Morocco are particularly robust and decorated with colourful spines.

Glossary of keywords

The cacti are listed according to their generic names.

The number of species is the number of officially described species of the respective genus, which, however, will vary over the course of time because of constant new discoveries and botanical reclassification.

Home: Origin and distribution are an important key to the correct care of the relevant species.

Body: This is a description of the shape of the body and the general appearance of the cacati.

Shape of growth: This will give you some information as to how the various genera will develop, even in old age, and whether they usually grow as solitary plants or produce off-

sets. This is an important aspect to consider when choosing the right plant container for repotting. Cacti which shoot vigorously and even form small cushions or clumps will, of course, require a much wider pot.

Spines: A brief overview of the huge variety of shapes and colours within one genus. It is hard to believe that nearly every cactus species has its own characteristic spines.

Flowers: In addition to information on which parts of the cactus will produce flowers, you will find notes on the size of the flower and the colour range of the genus. The individual flower generally blooms for two to three days, but can bloom either extremely briefly (one day or night) or even for a whole week.

Flowering time: The flowering period of a cactus can be very short in some species, which only produce a few flowers, or, in the case of profusely flowering species, can stretch from spring into summer. In general, in the latter case, the flowers will appear in several surges, depending on weather conditions. For example, *Mammillaria* may flower for weeks, during which "wreaths"

of flowers gradually push out of the axils.

Care: This includes special tips for the individual genera. Even within the same genus, requirements of care may vary greatly (for example, *Mammillaria, Opuntia*), so the instructions for care will always refer to the species recommended at the end of each generic description. A distinction is made between cacti grown on their own roots and those grafted on to others.

If overwintering is not mentioned as a special point, the general conditions are cool (5-10°C/41-50°F), bright and dry.

Propagating: This will always tell you the most advantageous method.

Recommended species: The suggestions are always for particularly beautiful species from the commonly available selection in most nurseries or garden centres, with the colour of the flower indicated in parentheses. When naming the recommended species, the genus name is always abbreviated and the species name written out in full.

Heliocereus speciosus is a climbing, bushy-growing cactus with slender shoots that comes from Mexico and Guatemala. It is an important parent plant of the Phyllocacti (Epiphyllum hybrids).

Astrophytum myriostigma, "bishop's mitre".

Astrophytum senile has densely growing spines.

Astrophytum

Astrophytum species ("star plants") are recognizable as a separate genus by the white to whitish-grey covering of fluff on their epidermis. The minute flakes of wool may cover the entire surface of the epidermis or appear only sporadically, or, in some cases, may even be missing altogether. The genus comprises six species with many variations depending on their locality and position.

Home: central and northern Mexico.

Body: flatly spherical, spherical to short-cylindrical. Usually 5-8 ribs, rarely less. Most are deep, in some species rounded off or flat (*A. asterias*), and their edges are often thickly beset with felty areoles, so they appear banded.

Shapes of growth: solitary growing, only rarely with offsets. In old age some species grow in a truncated column shape, with spirally turned ribs, up to 1 m tall (40 in).

Spines: some species have no spines, like *A. myriostigma* ("bishop's mitre") or *A. asterias* ("sea urchin cactus"). *A. ornatum* possesses 8 cm (3¼ in) long, bent, yellow (later greying), hard, sharp spines, while *A. capricorne* and *A. senile* have yellow, or brown to deep black (greying with old age),

paper-like, flattened, bent and twisted spines which erratically envelop the body of the cactus.

Flowers: appear centrally from new areoles at the top of the plant, often quite numerous. Up to 6 cm (2½ in) with a woolly tube that has scales with dark tips.

Colours: yellow, often with a brilliantly coloured orange to red/reddish-brown centre.

Flowering time: spring to summer.

Care: in loose, mainly mineral soil (for example, pumice gravel) with good fertilization, *Astrophytum* species will be ready to flower even when they are quite young plants. Grow

on their own rootstocks. Waterlogging should be strictly avoided.

Propagation: very easy, from seed.

Recommended species: all; only *A. coahuilense* is not suitable for beginners!

My tip: *Astrophytum* species can cross-breed very easily, so be careful with pollination.

Brasilicactus (Notocactus) haselbergii.

Cephalocereus senilis.

Brasilicactus

This genus comprises only two species, with some varieties, and is often described under the genus Notocactus (see p. 53).
Home: southern Brazil.
Body: flatly spherical, diameter up to 12 cm (4¾ in) and about 10-15 cm (4-6 in) high. Approximately 30 narrow, flat ribs with knobs with areoles.
Shapes of growth: mainly solitary.
Typical: depressed crown which, in older plants, is angled towards the direction of sunlight.
Spines: dense, fine, needle-like, glassy-transparent, whitish to golden yellow, about 1 cm (¾ in) long.

Flowers: appear centrally from the crown, usually numerous. Up to 3 cm (about 1¼ in), with a short funnel. The inner petals only partially open.
Colours: fiery red, red-orange to yellow-orange (B. haselbergii) or light green-yellowish (B. graessneri). Can self-pollinate!
Flowering time: early spring.
Care: very easy. Water well during the summer, likes humus-rich soil.
Propagation: very easily from seed. Reluctant to form offsets. Grafting unnecessary.
Recommended species: both are suitable for beginners.

Cephalocereus
(old man's head)

Only one species:
Cephalocereus senilis
(C. hoppenstedtii = Haseltonia)
Home: central Mexico.
Body: columns with 20-30 flat ribs and light green, greying epidermis. When it grows beyond 6 m (10 ft), it forms a pseudocephalium (see p. 8) with extremely densely placed woolly areoles.
Shapes of growth: solitary columns growing to heights of over 10 m (33 ft).
Spines: closely placed areoles with yellowish or grey spines and white, bristly hairs.
Flowers: appear at night,

from one side of the pseudocephalium. They are about 9 cm (3½ in) across, funnel-shaped, foul-smelling.
Colours: whitish, pink to pale yellowish.
Care: place the neck of the roots in coarse, permeable soil with a small amount of humus; fertilize well. In the summer, occasionally provide humid heat; frequent misting. No waterlogging!
Overwintering: bright, medium-warm temperatures (about 15°C/59° F), careful doses of water or light misting.
Propagation: very easy from seed. Low-growing grafts on to Trichocereus pachanoi flourish very well.

Cleistocactus

An easy-to-care-for genus (with over 50 species) which is very willing to flower once it has grown beyond a certain height (depending on the species, from 30-80 cm/12-32 in).
Home: central Peru, eastern Bolivia, northern Argentina, Paraguay, Uruguay (up to altitudes of 3,000 m/9,800 ft).
Body: slender columns. The shoots are slim to medium-thick (3-6 cm/1¼-2½ in) in diameter and multiple-ribbed.
Shape of growth: grows into long-shooting, large, bush-like structures. The shoots grow up to 1-2 m (40-80 in) tall; some even to 4 m/160 in.
Spines: densely packed, usually needle-like, thin.
Flowers: appear at the top of the body, are slim, with long tubes (up to 9 cm/3½ in) and stand almost straight up and away from the body. The petals at the tips hardly open up. The stigma protrudes considerably.
Colours: white, yellow, red to wine red, orange with red and red with green.
Flowering time: spring to early summer.
Care: water well during the summer. Grow it only on its own rootstock.
Propagation: easy, from offsets and seed.
Recommended species:
C. laniceps (red),
C. strausii (wine red),
C. wendlandiorum (orange; flowers when very young, from a height of about 15 cm/6 in).

Cleistocactus laniceps has white edge spines and brown yellow central spines.

Coryphantha pseudechina showing the honey glands.

Coryphantha sulcata without honey glands.

Coryphantha

This genus, like the *Mammillaria*, belongs to the group of warty cacti and comprises some 70 species. As with *Mammillaria*, the spiny areoles are situated at the tips of the warts or tubercles. The typical characteristic of *Coryphantha* cacti is the so-called "divided areole". It is thus named because a furrow runs along the top of the wart from the spiny areole almost to the axil. Many *Coryphantha* grow tough, dense, white axil wool which covers the crown of the cactus.

Home: from southern Canada across the entire USA to southern Mexico.

Body: spherical or long. Sometimes egg-shaped, rarely club-shaped. The warts are generally broad, large and blunt to longish and cone-shaped. There are two groups:

● *Recurvatae* which possesses honey-producing glands in the furrows or axils.

● *Sulcolanatae* without glands.

Shapes of growth: produces only few offsets and has a tendency to form small clumps. Maximum height: 15-20 cm (6-8 in).

Spines: Tough! The spines around the edges often envelop the cactus's body like rays. Often only one central spine which is straight or bent downward, rarely barbed. Edge spines: white, grey, yellow to brownish with dark tips. Central spines: brown to blackish, also with dark tips.

Flowers: appear centrally from the crown out of the new areoles' furrows. They are relatively large, up to 6 cm (2½ in) in diameter.

Colours: usually yellow, sometimes white, violet-pink through to deep red.

Flowering time: spring and summer.

Care: with correct care they flourish and produce many flowers.

During the growth phase: supply warmth, sunlight, plenty of light and water well. Recommended: a short summer rest period. Grows on its own rootstock, grafting unnecessary.

Propagation: easy from seed.

Recommended species: *C. elephantides* (white to deep red), *C. pseudechina* (violet-pink), *C. sulcata*, *C. sulcolanata* (both yellow).

Dolichothele uberiformis, a large-flowering species.

Echinocactus grusonii, "mother-in-law's armchair".

Dolichothele

This is a genus which is easy to grow and comprises thirteen species. It represents a sub-genus of *Mammillaria* (see p. 50).
Home: USA: Texas and central Mexico.
Body: spherical, *Mammillaria*-like, 3-15 cm (1¼-6 in) in diameter. Different-shaped tubercles, depending on the species, 8 mm-7 cm (⅜-2¾ in) long. Turnip-like root.
Shape of growth: vigorous growth of many shoots from the base, forms small cushions.
Spines: edge spines thin, white to pale yellow and pliable. The central spines stand out, are very sharp or barbed, strong yellow colouring or brownish.
Flowers: appear in rings near the crown, with long tubes out of the axils. Large-flowering species (for example, *D. longimamma*) with a length and diameter up to 6 cm (2½ in).
Colours: canary to sulphur yellow (often with slightly reddish tips) or whitish with a pink central stripe.
Flowering time: spring.
Care: soil: water-permeable and containing humus. In summer: in a bright, warm position with some moisture. Grows on its own rootstock.
Propagation: very easy from seed or offsets.
Recommended species: All are equally suitable.

Echinocactus

About ten species which all grow very large and do not flower until old.
Home: southern USA, central and northern Mexico.
Body: flatly spherical to spherical, multi-ribbed. The crown is very woolly.
Shape of growth: solitary, generally only forms offsets if injured. *E. grusonii* can grow to 1.5 m (5 ft) tall. *E. horizonthalonius* grows about 25 cm (10 in) tall.
Spines: tough and compact. The spines of *E. grusonii* are golden yellow, in new growth they are reddish-yellow. In other species they are brown, reddish-brown or amber, often with black tips.
Flowers: do not appear until the plants are quite old (exception: *E. horizonthalonius* which flowers when it is younger). The flowers grow from the thick wool on the crown.
Colours: straw yellow, pale to pinkish-violet.
Flowering time: summer.
Care: during the summer warm, sunny position; water and fertilize well. Overwinter at around 10ºC (50ºF) with minimum watering.
Propagation: easy, from seed.
Recommended species: *E. grusonii* (yellow; good for beginners), *E. horizonthalonius* (pink; requires hot, sunny position).

Echinocereus palmeri belongs to the pectinate species.

"Green" Echinocereae which remain small.

Echinocereus

Popular genus comprising about 80 species.
Home: south-western USA and Mexico.
Body: two groups can be distinguished:

"Green", loosely spined species with a maximum of twelve ribs. Their shape varies from long, thin, squarish, prostrate to fat, ungainly and long-cylindrical.

Densely spined (so-called pectinate) species. They have more than twelve ribs, are squarer and are thickly beset with areoles with no gaps.
Shape of growth: up to m (40 in) tall; most shoot vigorously from the base.

Spines: in "green" species: dagger-like, two colours, up to 8 cm (3 in) long. In pectinate species, they are shorter and arranged in a comb-like order. There are also bristly and hairy species (E. longisetus, E. delaetii).
Colours: white, yellow, grey to brown and black in the "green" species. In pectinate species, very colourful, yellowish-red, red, reddish-brown, often arranged in a ring shape and changing colour.
Flowers: appear along the sides of the body. Typical: the tube is covered in needle-like spines, the stigma is always green. Size: up to 12 cm (4 in).

Colours: white, yellow, orange to brilliant red. Pectinate species: usually light pink to deep violet, often with a green or white ring. A few have greenish-yellow flowers with a brown central stripe.
Flowering time: from early spring into the summer, depending on the species.
Care: mineral soil. In summer: airy (outside), sunny with plenty of watering. Misting during the evening hours. From the end of the first month of autumn, stop watering.
Overwintering: constantly cool (5-10°C/41-50°F), bright and completely dry. The cacti often shrink a great deal, but fill out again quickly in the spring.

Propagation: very easy, from seed and offsets.
Recommended species: all. If you have limited space, it is better to choose the pectinate species as they do not shoot so vigorously. The bristled or hairy species are sensitive to too much moisture.

1. Echinocereus durangensis.
2. Echinocereus salmdyckianus; together with E. scheerii (pink) the first of the Echinocereae to flower in spring.
3. Echinocereus moricalli shrinks most conspicuously during winter dormancy and does not fill out again completely until all its flowers have withered.

Echinofossulocactus lamellosus, a typical representative of this species.

Echinofossulocactus albatus is one of the few yellow-flowering species.

Echinofossulocactus

These "lamella" cacti are meadow-dwellers, of which about 30 species are known to date.

Home: central Mexican mountainous regions.

Body: spherical with about 10-100 deep, angular, usually wavy ribs.

Shape of growth: many remain spherical, some tend to stretch in old age and produce short columnar shapes. In youth, most grow solitary, but shoot vigorously in old age.

Spines: sparse or dense, depending on the species. Edge spines: white, thin.

Central spines: tough, long, often curved like horns. The central spine is directed upwards and is flattened, short, dagger-like or up to 8 cm (3¼ in) long, wavy or spiral.

Flowers: appear centrally on the crown. Up to 4 cm (under 2 in). Only rarely protrude from the spines.

Colours: whitish to bluish-violet with a darker stripe in the centre, or yellow, whitish to cream with a dark stripe along the back.

Flowering time: early spring.

Care: humus-rich soil, water-permeable. During the summer, water well and fertilize. Will also flourish in bright positions with little sunlight.

Propagation: very easy, from seed. *NB:* the various species cross very easily among themselves. Grow only on their own rootstocks.

Recommended species: all are good for beginners.

Eriocactus magnificus has densely set areoles.

Ferocactus glaucescens starts flowering at five years.

Eriocactus

This genus comprises four species and counts as a sub-genus of Notocactus.
Home: southern Brazil, Paraguay.
Body: spherical to begin with, later column-like (up to 1 m/40 in tall), blue green. The crown grows at an angle to face the light and is covered in wool.
Shape of growth: body 10-15 cm (4-6 in) thick, produces offsets even when young.
Spines: the edge spines are fine, thin, bristly, also hairy. White, later greying, up to 1 cm (¾ in) long. The central spines, depending on the species, are tough, needle-like, soft, even bristly. Golden yellow to yellow brown.
Flowers: appear centrally from the crown wool. 5-6 cm (2-2½ in), funnel shaped, the petals are conspicuously rounded, the stigma and stamens are the same colour.
Colours: light to dark yellow.
Flowering time: spring to summer.
Care: soil: nutritious, good permeability, slightly humus-containing. Grow on their own rootstocks. In summer: constant moisture; in great heat, semi-shady position.
Propagation: easy, from seed and offsets.
Recommended species: all.

Ferocactus

There are 35 species, most of which do not flower until they are old.
Home: south-western states of the USA, Mexico.
Body: flatly spherical, spherical to slightly column-like in their youth. In old age up to 3 m (120 in) tall. Have eleven to 25 deep, angular ribs (depending on species).
Epidermis: tough, dark green to blue green.
Shape of growth: usually solitary, does not produce offsets until old.
Exception: *F. robustus* and *F. flavovirens* which produce offsets in their youth.
Spines: usually very tough, yellow, greenish, and brilliant orange to red.
Flowers: numerous in older plants, as a ring around the crown. Up to 5 cm (2 in), short funnel.
Colours: usually yellow, sometimes orange to purple violet.
Flowering time: spring to summer.
Care: nutrient-rich, water-permeable soil. In summer: sunny, water well.
Propagation: from seed.
Recommended species: *F. glaucescens* (yellow), *F. latispinus* (whitish to pink, called "devil's tongue" on account of the broad, red, central spine), both flower from the age of five to six years. *F. stainesii* (orange red), *F. wislizenii* (yellow to orange).

Gymnocalycium baldianum from Argentina.

Gymnocalycium uruguayense.

Gymnocalycium

Produces many large flowers; a genus highly recommended for beginners, comprising over 80 species.

Home: southern Brazil, Bolivia, Argentina, Uruguay, Paraguay.

Body: flatly spherical to spherical, only few species are cylindrical. Well-defined, separate, broad ribs (depending on the species, 8-15 ribs). Often have nose-like protuberances or cross furrows between the areoles. The colour of the body ranges from light to dark green, green grey and brownish.

Shape of growth: only few grow solitary, most form offsets at the base. About 20 cm (8 in) tall with a diameter of 15 cm (6 in).

Spines: *Gymnocalycium* cacti can be divided into two groups, depending on the type of spines:

● Species with more or less closely growing spines. The spines are thin and stiff and are often arranged over the body in the shape of spiders. They are yellow to greyish-white with a reddish-brown base from only a few millimetres up to 4 cm (1½ in) long. Most are bent downwards; no central spine.

● Species with protruding spines. These spines possess one or several central spines which are often missing in young plants.

Colours: yellow, whitish, brown to black.

Flowers: appear centrally from the crown, often even on three-year-old plants. The tube is short, slim, naked and covered with bare scales, which gives them the name *Gymnocalycium* = the "ones with the naked calyx". Flowers: diameter up to 6 cm (2½ in).

Colours: vary from white (often with a red throat), cream to yellow, pink to deep red and wine red.

Flowering time: spring to summer.

Care: as most of these species are meadow dwellers, they do not have to be exposed to full sunlight. Water well during the summer; they can also be kept outside if sheltered from rain. Growing them on their own rootstocks is recommended. Only graft the yellow and red chlorophyll-free mutations of *G. mihanovichii* (see photo, p. 13).

Propagation: very easy, from seed or offsets.

Recommended species: all, particularly, *G. andreae* (yellow), *G. baldianum* (red-violet), *G. bruchii* (pink), *G. denudatum* (white to yellowish), *G. multiflorum* (pink to pinkish-orange), *G. quehlianum* (white with a red throat), *G. uruguayense* (whitish, yellow).

Lobivia rebutioides with spines in a comb-like (pectinate) arrangement.

Lobivia

The name Lobivia is an anagram of the name Bolivia, the main distribution area of this extensive genus, which comprises some 106 recognized species with many varieties and other numerous, as yet undescribed, species.

Home: Bolivia, Peru, Argentina and Chile.

Body: spherical to short, column-shaped with many ribs (depending on the species, 12-30 ribs), which are divided up into narrow, angular protuberances. Grows to a maximum height of 30 cm (12 in); diameter rarely over 10 cm (4 in).

Shape of growth: most species form lots of offsets and clumps or cushions.

Spines: depending on the species, they can be thin, pliable, sharp, hard, bristly, short and close to the body or very long, slightly curved, sometimes with long barbs. The edge spines almost envelop the body and, depending on the species, they are coloured yellow to brown and blackish-grey. The central spines can be long and curved or shaped like fish hooks and be up to 8 cm (3¼ in) long and directed upwards.

Flowers: appear on the sides of the body from older areoles. They have short to long tubes and are relatively large (up to 10 cm/4 in long and 6-10 cm/2½ 4 in in diameter). The tube is usually densely covered with wool or hair.

Colours: yellow, fiery red-yellow, orange to tomato red, pink to lilac, often with a lighter or darker throat.

Flowering time: spring to summer.

Care: soil should be loose and contain humus. In summer: water well, if possible provide intense sunlight (promotes proper growth of spines!) and plenty of fresh air. In the autumn: spray to toughen up the plant. Overwintering: definitely cool (5-10°C/41-50°F), bright and dry. Only then will these species be willing to flower profusely. Grow only on their own rootstocks. Choose a tall, wide plant container in which the turnip-like roots and the numerous offsets will have enough room.

Propagation: very easy, from seed and offsets.

Recommended species: *L. backebergiana* (orange, see photo. p. 28), *L. rebutioides* and *L. famatimensis* (both with large, yellow flowers and attractive spines standing in comb-like arrangements), *L. jajoiana* (tomato red), *L. pentlandii* (white, yellow, pink to violet, see photo, p. 3) and *L. wrightiana* (pink, with attractive, long, barbed spines).

49

Mammillaria

This genus contains over 350 species and many varieties. The name is derived from the Latin *mamma* = *mamilla* = nipple, teat or tubercle (wart). Instead of ribs, all *Mammillaria* possess tubercles. There are spiny areoles at the tips of the tubercles and again in the axils in the depressions between the tubercles. The offsets and the flowers grow out of the axils. The tubercles are arranged in spirals all round the body.

Home: southern USA, Mexico, Guatemala, Honduras, the West Indian islands to Venezuela and Colombia.

Body: flatly spherical, slim or thick columns.

Shape of growth: most species produce lots of offsets and form cushions. Only a few grow solitary. The larger species may be up to 50 cm (20 in) tall, the dwarf species only a few centimetres.

Spines: straight, curved, barbed, feathered, comblike, pliable or stiff.

Colours: white, yellow, red, brown or black.

Flowers: small, usually appear in a ring around the crown area out of the axils grown the previous year.

Colours: whitish, cream-coloured, yellowish, pink, carmine red to dark lilac.

Flowering time: spring.

Care: see p. 17.

Propagation: easy, from seed or offsets.

Recommended species: all. These cacti are the most willing to flower and grow.

Mammillaria carmenae – forgotten for a long time and then rediscovered.

Mediolobivia rauschii forms attractive small clumps.

Neochilenia paucicostata is also called Pyrrhocactus.

Mediolobivia

A genus which remains quite small but flowers profusely, with about seventeen species and many varieties.

Home: the mountainous regions of the Andes (northern Argentina, Bolivia).

Body: short-cylindrical, diameter generally 2-4 cm (¾-1½in), height up to 8 cm (3¼in). Ribs, 10-15, mostly flat.

Shape of growth: dwarf cacti which produce lots of offsets and form small cushions.

Spines: usually weak, fine, light-glassy to whitish-yellow.

Flowers: appear numerously all round the body. Funnel-shaped, up to 5 cm (2 in).

Colours: yellow to dark yellow, orange, orange red, carmine red, salmon pink. The stigma is typically green for this genus or yellowy green.

Flowering time: spring.

Care: permeable, humusrich soil. Can be grown on its own rootstock or as a graft. In summer: water well, sunny position, plenty of fresh air. Spray.

Propagation: very easy, from seed or offsets.

Recommended species: all suitable for the beginner, particularly:
M. aureiflora (yellow),
M. rauschii (orange),
M. ritteri (cinnabar red).

Neochilenia

This genus includes 55 species which, in their original habitat, will retract into their large turnip-like roots in times of drought.

Home: Chile.

Body: spherical to shortcylindrical. The epidermis is reddish, dark brown to blackish, rarely light green.

Shape of growth: remains small, from 5 cm to 15 cm tall (2-6 in), with a diameter of 5 cm (2 in).

Spines: in larger species mainly black, grey, tough, long, straight or lightly curved towards the body. In smaller species, the spines lie close to the body, are stiff and very short, some have white hairs which envelop the body.

Flowers: appear centrally from the crown of the cactus. Funnel-shaped, to about 5 cm (2 in).

Colours: whitish, creamcoloured, pink, yellow, orange, copper.

Flowering time: early in the spring to summer.

Care: Mineral soil. In the summer: warm and sunny position. Indoors, better grown as a graft.

Propagation: from seed. Grafting or offsets easier.

Recommended species:
N. hankeana (creamy white),
N. mitis (creamy yellow),
N. occulta (pale golden yellow),
N. paucicostata (reddishwhite).

Neoporteria gerocephala has a long tube.

Nopalxochia phyllanthoides "Deutsche Kaiserin".

Neoporteria

Approximately 22 species.
Home: Chile.
Body: spherical, takes the shape of short columns in old age; about 15-20 cm (6-8 in) tall and 10 cm (4 in) thick. Deeply furrowed ribs with densely placed areoles.
Shape of growth: solitary, only rarely forms offsets.
Spines: very varied. Black, tough, slightly curved, or straight, about 4 cm (1¾ in) long bristle spines or 2-3 cm (¾- 1¼ in) long straight, tough, amber-coloured spines; others may be light yellow, whitish-grey, yellow, grey or black-tipped, or have long bristle spines which envelop the body.

Flowers: appear from the crown area. The outer petals open wide or roll back, the inner petals remain almost shut, so that the stigma and the stamens can hardly be seen.
Colours: red, white to straw-coloured, with red or pink tips.
Flowering time: winter and early spring.
Care: mineral soil, grows on its own rootstock. In summer: warm, sunny position, water well.
Propagation: very easy, from seed.
Recommended species: *N. gerocephala* (carmine pink), *N. rapifera, N. subgibbosa, N. villosa* (all white with red/pink tips).

Nopalxochia

These foliage cacti are tree dwellers (epiphytes) in their countries of origin, and are reliable, profusely flowering cacti.
Two species: *N. ackermannii* and *N. phyllanthoides.*
We generally grow hybrids of these two wild species.
Home: Mexico.
Body: long stalks. The leaves are flat, two-edged, up to 30 cm (12 in) long.
Shape of growth: pendulous and bushy, produces shoots mainly from the base.
Spines: none.
Flowers: appear from the small areoles along the edges of the leaves.

Flowers up to 10 cm (4 in).
Colours: whitish-pink to light pinkish-red.
Flowering time: early spring.
Care: requires very nutrient-rich and humus-rich soil. Grows only on its own rootstock. In summer: keep the soil constantly moist, if possible keep it outside. Semi-shady position! Fertilize well.
Overwintering: bright, warm (15-20°C/59-68°F) and dry.
Propagation: the best method is with a proper cutting.
Recommended species: all wild types and hybrids.

Notocactus

Plants that flower profusely. There are sixteen species and numerous varieties.

Home: Argentina, Uruguay and southern Brazil.

Body: spherical to short column-like, height and diameter from about 15-20 cm (6-8 in). Ribs (depending on the species, 10-40), deeply furrowed and angular with nose-shaped protuberances.

Shape of growth: usually no offsets until later years.

Spines: short, rayed, others are longer, yellowish, reddish-brown to black, thin, pliable, growing close to the body or ray-like white edge spines with longer, dark reddish-brown central spines.

Flowers: appear around the crown areoles. Up to 8 cm (3¼ in), funnel-shaped.

Colours: light to dark yellow, copper, deep pink to wine red. The stigma is always pink to purple red

Flowering time: spring to summer.

Care: nutrient-rich soil, containing humus. In summer: water well and fertilize. During flowering, stand them in very sunny positions as the flowers often only open completely when the sunlight is intense.

Propagation: easy from seed; in some species from offsets.

Recommended species: N. apricus, N. concinnus, N. ottonis (all yellow), N. rutilans (pink carmine), N. submammulosus (yellow), N. uebelmannianus (wine to violet red).

Notocactus uebelmannianus also produces yellow flowers.

Notocactus concinnus is ideal for the windowsill: it remains small and flowers profusely.

Opuntia hystricina var. bensonii.

Parodia mairanana, suitable for beginners.

Opuntia
(fig cactus)

A very undemanding, very fast-growing genus with over 300 species.
Home: in all cactus regions.
Body: single, round or oval, thick, fleshy leaf-like bodies, up to 30 cm (12 in) long. Often intensely blue green.
Shape of growth: prostrate, bushy or tree-like (up to 12 m/39 ft tall). Can produce offsets from all areoles.
Spines: needle-like, tough with tiny, hardly visible barbs, or colourful, flattened and paper-like, or white and bristly.
Flowers: usually appear from the areoles along the edges of the leaves. Cup-shaped, up to 10 cm (4 in), without a tube.
Colours: yellow, orange to red, yellow red, deep pink, rarely white.
Flowering time: spring to summer.
Care: nutrient-rich, sandy soil. In the summer plenty of sunlight and warmth, water well and fertilize. Also suitable for large containers.
Propagation: very easy from offsets, but a bit more time-consuming than from seed.
Recommended species: *O. azurea* (red yellow), *O. microdasys* (yellow) *O. hystricina var. bensonii* (hardy).

Parodia

Parodia remain small and will start to flower as three-year-old seedlings. There are 87 species with many varieties.
Home: southern Brazil, Bolivia, Paraguay and northern Argentina.
Body: flatly spherical, spherical to cylindrical (maximum of 8 cm/3¼ in wide to 20 cm/8 in tall). There are 13-24 ribs, depending on the species, which run spirally, and are formed as rows of tubercles.
Shape of growth: may be solitary or clump-forming.
Spines: edge spines are thin, white to yellow, and envelop the body entirely. Central spines are darker and usually tougher.
Flowers: appear centrally from the usually woolly crown. Bell- or funnel-shaped, up to 4 cm (1½ in)
Colours: yellow, yellow orange to copper and red.
Flowering time: spring to summer.
Care: fine, porous, slightly humus-containing soil. In summer: do not water much but fertilize; bright position with plenty of fresh air, protected if under glass.
Propagation: very simple, from an offset. Propagation from seed is extremely time-consuming.
Recommended species: *P. chrysacanthion* (yellow), *P. maassii* (red), *P. mutabilis* (yellow orange), *P. sanguiniflora* (deep red).

Phyllocacti – weeks of splendid flowers.

Pseudolobivia ancistrophora opens its flowers at night.

Phyllocactus hybrids
(*Epiphyllum* hybrids)

Hybrids were created by crossing *Heliocereus, Nopalxochia, Selenicereus* and others; the present-day name is *Epiphyllum*. About twenty species and some 10,000 hybrids.
Home: southern Mexico to the tropical areas of South America.
Body: like leaf cacti. Flat or three- to four-sided branches from 40-100 cm (16-40 in) long. Small areoles in the notches of the leaf edges.
Shapes of growth: bushy.
Spines: none, or very few.
Flowers: appear from the areoles. Diameter up to 25 cm (10 in).
Colours: white, yellow, orange, pink, all shades of red to violet.
Flowering time: spring.
Care: nutrient-rich soil with plenty of humus. Requires large, stable plant containers as the branches often droop. In summer: water well and fertilize regularly. Ideal for outside or in semi-shade (the branches will turn reddish in sunlight). Overwintering: 8-15ºC (46-59ºF), bright to semi-shady, water sparingly but avoid further growth. Only grown on its own rootstock.
Propagation: easy from cuttings of year-old leaves.
Recommended species: all.

Pseudolobivia

Problem-free, very willing to flower; about 24 species. Every species possesses characteristics of both *Echinopsis* and *Lobivia,* either in the shape of the body or the type and colour of the flowers.
Home: northern Argentina to eastern Bolivia.
Body: usually flatly spherical with 16-30 ribs.
Shape of growth: solitary globular cacti, form very few offsets.
Spines: very varied. The edge spines lie close to the body or are directed outwards, grey, yellow to dark brown, very sharp. The central spines are thin and often have a hook; whitish to yellow, grey to black.
Flowers: appear from older areoles, up to 18 cm (7 in) long and almost 10 cm (4 in) in diameter.
Colours: white, often with a pink edge or intensely yellow or red to dark carmine red.
Flowering time: spring to summer.
Care: nutritious soil, containing humus; outdoors preferably sheltered from rain, without exposure to intense sunlight.
Propagation: easy, from seed.
Recommended species: *P. ancistrophora* (white), *P. aurea* (yellow), *P. kermesina* (carmine red).

Rebutia minuscala (red), Rebutia violaciflora (violet), Rebutia marsoneri (yellow) and brilliantly coloured hybrids.

Rebutia

I can recommend *Rebutia* for any beginner. This is a charming, colourfully flowering genus of cacti that are happy to grow and produce offsets, with species (approximately nineteen) and varieties that do not become very large and will, therefore, fit on any windowsill.

Home: northern Argentina to north-eastern Bolivia.

Body: squat and spherical, possesses spirally arranged ribs beginning at the depressed crown, which are completely disguised by being covered in small, flat tubercles. The maximum diameter is about 8 cm (3¼ in), and their height is generally less than that.

Shape of growth: remain small and produce many offsets; generally rapidly form small clumps.

Spines: these protrude from small, white, felty areoles and completely envelop the body radially. They are fine, needle-like, thin, bristly and coloured light-glassy to whitish, white, yellow, yellowish to brownish. The edge spines and central spines are indistinguishable. In some species the entire body of the cactus is covered (with up to 35 spines around each areole).

Flowers: appear from the base up to the top third of the circumference of the body, in rings from the areoles. They are small and funnel-shaped, the narrow tube has a few scales but is mainly bare. The flowers may attain a diameter of 2-5 cm (¾-2 in) and often appear so profusely, radially, that they entirely cover the body of the cactus.

Colours: range from light to dark yellow, orange, pink to violet and brilliant red (even a white hybrid has been created).

Flowering time: spring.

Care: mineral soil, with little humus and good water-permeability. Only grows on its own rootstock. In summer: sunny position, plenty of fresh air, water well and fertilize.

Propagation: problem-free from offsets or from seed. The new plants grown from offsets will produce flowers as early as the age of two or three years. Some species are self-pollinating and often produce seeds after flowering, which will fall on to the soil and, without much care, begin to germinate. Seedlings will usually flourish very well like this.

Recommended species: all, particularly,
R. marsoneri (yellow),
R. violaciflora (violet,
R. senilis with several varieties (yellow and red, with attractive white spines).

Schlumbergera truncata.

Selenicereus grandiflorus, "Queen of the Night".

Schlumbergera
hybrids
Christmas cactus

These are epiphytes which were created by crossing *Schlumbergera* and *Zygocactus*.
Home of the pure species: Brazil.
Body: leaf-like, multi-branching flat shoots.
Shape of growth: bushy.
Spines: fine, yellow to brown bristles.
Flowers: appear from the areoles of the shoot tips.
Colours: white, yellow, orange, red, pink violet.
Flowering time: early to midwinter (sometimes in early spring).
Care: porous soil, sandy, some humus. Repot after flowering. After the flowers are over, It observes a short dormancy period, then the growth phase commences. In summer: if possible place outside but in semi-shade, keep it moist and fertilize regularly. Towards the end of the first month of autumn take it back inside where reduced light will promote the formation of buds. In autumn and winter: 17-20°C (63-68°F); keep the plants in the same position or they will not form any buds. Water regularly but do not fertilize.
Propagation: very easy, from one to two-year-old leaf cuttings.
Recommended species: all.

Selenicereus

About 24 species with splendid flowers (15-40 cm/6-16 in).
Home: southern Texas, eastern Mexico, central America, West Indies to the northern coast of South America.
Body: up to several metres long, shoots with 4-8 ribs. Aerial roots.
Shape of growth: climbing, branching and bush-like.
Spines: short, around small areoles, glassy yellow, inconspicuous, often missing altogether.
Flowers: appear on the oldest shoots from the areoles. Open at dusk, bloom at night and wither the following morning. Scent of vanilla. The inner petals: white, bell-like, broad. Outer petals: golden yellow to reddish-brown, stand out radially.
Flowering time: end of spring and summer.
Care: as for epiphytes (see p. 25). Soil containing humus, nutrient-rich, well-aerated. In summer: warm, semi-shady position, water regularly and fertilize well. Overwintering: 10-15°C (50-59°F), medium watering but avoid starting up new growth.
Propagation: from offsets, cuttings or seed.
Recommended species: *S. grandiflorus*, *S. macdonaldiae* (largest flowers), *S. pteranthus* ("Princess of the Night").

Sulcorebutia crispata with extremely attractive spination.

Weingartia neocuminigii var. keohresii.

Sulcorebutia

Over 40 species.
Home: Bolivia between 2,000 and 3,000 m (6,500-9,800 ft).
Body: flatly spherical to short cylindrical, 3-4 cm (1¼-1½ in) in diameter with robust, turnip-like roots. Spirally arranged ribs with flat protuberances.
Shape of growth: most species produce offsets.
Spines: longish areoles with edge spines that are radial and curved slightly towards the body; they are short, tough, white, yellow or reddish-brown to black. The central spines are tough, straight, the same colour or slightly darker.
Flowers: appear all around the body, usually on the lower to middle part; funnel-shaped.
Colours: yellow, orange, red, pink to dark violet.
Flowering time: spring.
Care: mineral soil, a little humus, very water-permeable. Grow on their own rootstocks. Plenty of fresh air and sunshine, water and fertilize carefully.
Propagation: easy, from offsets and from seed. The offsets will start flowering as early as the following year.
Recommended species: all, particularly, *S. crispata* (violet), *S. kruegeri* (golden yellow to orange), *S. rauschii* (pink), *S. steinbachii* (red to red violet), *S. tiraquensis* (purple).

Weingartia

About fifteen species.
Home: the Andes of Bolivia and northern Argentina between 2,400 and 3,200 m (7,800-10,490 ft)
Body: flat to elongated spherical with short turnip-like roots. The ribs are spirally arranged and divided into protuberances.
Shape of growth: can become about 15 cm (6 in) thick and 20 cm (8 in) tall but will not produce offsets until quite old.
Spines: compactly arranged, robust, up to 30 spines per areole, with edge and central spines often very similar.
Colours: white, yellow to light brown with brown to black tips.
Flowers: appear very numerously in rings from the areoles around the crown. Relatively small (up to 3 cm/1 in).
Colours: canary yellow to orange red.
Flowering time: spring.
Care: mineral soil, very little humus but very permeable. Grows on own rootstock. In summer: very sunny position; water and fertilize regularly.
Propagation: easy from seed and offsets.
Recommended species: all, particularly, *W. cumingii, W. lanata, W. longigibba, W. neocumingii* (all yellow), *W. neocumingii var. koehresii* (orange).

Thelocactus

A genus with approximately nineteen species, colourful spination and splendid flowers.

Home: from Mexico to Texas.

Body: spherical, stretched to short cylindrical. The ribs are divided up into large, often hexagonal, tubercles, with spined areoles at their tips.

Shape of growth: usually solitary, only a few species form offsets at their bases.

Spines: often tough and colourful. The central spines are often longer, flattened, pliable and rough. Alternatively: broad with long rills, curved, stiff and sharp.

Colours: white, yellow, red, patchy red yellow, brown or grey.

Flowers: appear centrally from the areoles of the crown. Bell-shaped to funnel-shaped, diameter up to 6 cm (2½ in).

Colours: white, pink to deep red, purple pink with a white ring and a red throat.

Flowering time: spring to late summer.

Care: soil, mainly mineral, very little humus. Grows on its own rootstock. In summer: warm and very sunny position, water and fertilize plentifully and regularly.

Propagation: very easy, from seed or offsets.

Recommended species: *T. bicolor* (purple pink with a red throat), *T. beuckii* (dark red), *T. conothelos* (purple violet), *T. hexaedrophorus* (silky white).

Thelocactus conothelos remains spherical even in old age.

Thelocactus bueckii with hexagonal tubercles and bizarrely shaped spines.

Index

Figures in bold indicate illustrations.

Index

Index

Cover photographs
Front cover: *Orchid cactus; Opuntia ficus-indica; Queen of the night; Echinocactus grusonii.*
Inside front cover: *Pseudolobivia ancistrophora.* Inside back cover: *Bed of cacti in the author's greenhouse.*
Back cover: *Echinocactus grusonii.*

Photographic acknowledgements
Cover photography L. Rose;
Becherer: inside front cover, p. 2, 3, 5, 11 Nos. 2, 4, 6, 7, 8, 9; p. 21, 27, 28 Nos. 2-9; p. 30, 31, 33, 41, 42, 43, 44, 45, 46, 47, 48 r., 50, 51 r., 52, 53, 54, 55, 58, 59; Busek: p. 7, 11 no. 5; p. 14, 19, 24, 28 No. 1; p. 39, 48; Eisenbeiss: front cover, inside back cover, p. 11 No. 1, 3; p. 13, 40, 49, 51 l., 56, 57.

© 1989 Gräfe und Unzer GmbH, Munich

Reprinted 1998.

This edition published 1994 by
Merehurst Limited
Ferry House, 51-57 Lacy Road,
Putney, London SW15 1PR
Reprinted 1995

ISBN 1 85391 322 7

All rights reserved. No part of this publication may be reproduced, stored in a retrieval system, or transmitted in any form or by any means, electronic, mechanical, photocopying, recording or otherwise, without the prior written permission of both the copyright owner and the publisher of this book.

A catalogue record for this book is available from the British Library.

English text copyright ©
Merehurst Limited 1994
Translated by Astrid Mick
Edited by Lesley Young
Design and typesetting by Cooper Wilson Design
Illustrations by Marlene Gemke
Printed in Hong Kong by Wing King Tong.

3 0132 01900614 2

The home of WEA North–East Region:
Joseph Cowen House, 21 Portland Terrace,
Newcastle-upon-Tyne

The Right to Learn:

the WEA in the North of England 1910-2010

Edited by Jonathan Brown

First published in the United Kingdom in 2010 by: WEA
Reg. Office: Workers' Educational Association, 4 Luke Street, London, EC2A 4XW

Publishing consultants: Northern Heritage Services Limited

Text and photographs
The Centenary Book Working Group and acknowledged suppliers.

Andrew Palmer of Inspired Design designed the book's cover
(e-mail: info@inspireddesign.co.uk; web address: www.inspireddesign.co.uk).

Front cover:
T&GWU residential summer school for women trade unionists, 1959 (WEA National Archive); course organisers and tutors, 2008
(WEA North-East Region);
Durham summer school, 1921 (WEA Collection, Tyne and Wear Archives); WEA Climate Change Conference, 2008 (WEA North-East Region);
Philip Brown — pre-First World War tutor (Imperial War Museum); Frances and Albert Mansbridge circa 1910 (WEA National Archive).
Back cover:
Liz Armstrong, Skeff Vaughan and Victor Cadaxa (WEA North-East Region); Campaigning Alliance for Lifelong Learning, 2008 (Jane Atkins, UCU).

Design and layout: Ian Scott Design

Printed and bound in China by Latitude Press Limited

British Library Cataloguing in Publication Data.
A catalogue record of this book is available from the British Library.

ISBN 978-0-900823-89-3

All Rights Reserved.
No part of this publication may be reproduced in any form or by any means – graphic, electronic or mechanical including photocopying, recording, taping or information storage and retrieval
systems – without prior permission in writing by the publisher. The Publisher makes no representation, express or implied with regard to the accuracy of the information in this book and
cannot accept any legal responsibility for any errors or omissions that have been made.

The production of this book has been generously assisted by funding from the Trusthouse Charitable Foundation, the History Workshop Trust and Lord Jeremy Beecham.

Contents